Praise for
The Coaching Effect

"Using evidence-based findings and vivid examples, Bill Eckstrom and Sarah Wirth reveal the 'missing piece' in leadership: the coaching factor. They show how, using growth rings and healthy tension, you can get the great people you hired to perform at peak capacity."

—MARY UHL-BIEN, Ph.D., BNSF Railway Endowed Professor
of Leadership, Texas Christian University

"An interesting and fact-based read that teaches how high-performance coaching creates real business value."

—KAREN FLYNN, Senior Vice President and
Chief Commercial Officer, West Pharmaceutical Services

"Unbelievably practical information backed by extensive research. Every single leader who is willing to change the nature of their communication to the coaching style so clearly laid out by Bill and Sarah will increase the rapport they have with their team and results. If you lead sales folks then this is a must read and implement."

—PETER JENSEN, Ph.D., Canadian Olympic Sport Psychologist;
Founder, Performance Coaching Inc.

"We have used the train the trainer methodology for years in Special Operations, coaching the coach with these tools and data is a must-have for all leaders."

—COMMANDER JACK RIGGINS, Navy SEAL (Ret.)

"Working in the high-performance mindset field with elite coaches and teams I can tell you this book is spot on about what creates and sustains growth. I can say with absolute certainty—read this book and you will become a better coach, a better leader, and a better human being."

—LARRY WIDMAN, M.D., High-Performance Mindset Coach;
Cofounder, Performance Mountain

"Bill Eckstrom and Sarah Wirth are clearly the brightest minds in the field of sales coaching. The advice in this book is priceless. It should be mandatory reading for anyone who is in charge of a sales team, or any customer facing team. If you want to grow sales, this book will help you win."

—GERHARD GSCHWANDTNER,
Founder and Publisher, *Selling Power* magazine

"I've read dozens of books on 'how to play' the sales game. *Finally*, we have seminal research and observations about what is required to extract high-sales performance in a compelling and practical approach. If you're a sales leader now or want to know how to assess a good leader, this is the playbook we've been waiting for. A big Gatorade shower for Bill and Sarah. Bravo!"

—RUSS PASTENA, Senior Vice President,
Global Head of Sales Operations and Enablement

"There are about as many sales books as there are salespeople, but nothing else on the shelf compares to *The Coaching Effect*. It will have a long lasting effect on me and mine."

—JOHN ROOD, Senior Vice President, Marketing,
Disney Channels Worldwide

"Bill and Sarah are the real deal. Their guidance has added a new dimension to our sales leadership that is missing in most organizations!"

—KAREN M. GUSTIN, LLIF, Ameritas®,
Executive Vice President – Group Division

"Eckstrom and Wirth help you rethink coaching effectiveness and growth. Using research and data-driven methods, they honed their approach to coaching by considering the perspective of the coach, the coachee, and whether it delivered results. The outcome is insightful and proven-effective. Check out the discomfort factor (unexpected), the Growth Rings and how they fuel the Coaching Performance Equation, how to consider both the quantity and quality of coaching, and their simple but effective 4-step coaching process. If you want to improve coaching and organization performance, this is the right book for you."

—MIKE KUNKLE, founder, Sales Transformation Architect, Transforming Sales Results, LLC

"Bill and Sarah do an excellent job of applying systems thinking principles to their method of coaching for performance improvement. I teach these same scientific-based principles to my MBA class on Leading Change every semester. Bill's 2017 TEDxUniversityofNevada talk provides valuable support material for the book. Highly recommend!"

—BRET L. SIMMONS, Ph.D., Associate Professor of Management, College of Business, University of Nevada

"The objective and data-driven focus on the value of effective coaching on sales growth makes this book an excellent read."

—KEVIN SIEBERT, President, Tecumseh Poultry LLC

"*The Coaching Effect* makes a compelling and evidence-based case for ambitious future leaders learning how to coach and embrace discomfort."

—YANNICK JACOB, Existential Coach and FMR Programme Leader, MSc Coaching Psychology, University of East London

"A leader's ability to coach is no longer a nice-to-have and is now a must-have."

—TOM OLSON, Chairman and CEO, Points West Community Bank, Windsor, CO

THE
COACHING
EFFECT

WHAT GREAT LEADERS DO TO
INCREASE SALES, ENHANCE
PERFORMANCE, AND SUSTAIN GROWTH

BILL ECKSTROM &
SARAH WIRTH

GREENLEAF
BOOK GROUP PRESS

Published by Greenleaf Book Group Press
Austin, Texas
www.gbgpress.com

Distributed by Greenleaf Book Group

For ordering information or special discounts for bulk purchases, please contact Greenleaf Book Group at PO Box 91869, Austin, TX 78709, 512.891.6100.

Design and composition by Greenleaf Book Group and Kim Lance
Cover design by Greenleaf Book Group and Kim Lance
Cover Image: © Shutterstock / Andrew Krasovitckii

Publisher's Cataloging-in-Publication data is available.

Print ISBN: 978-1-62634-609-3

eBook ISBN: 978-1-62634-610-9

Part of the Tree Neutral® program, which offsets the number of trees consumed in the production and printing of this book by taking proactive steps, such as planting trees in direct proportion to the number of trees used: www.treeneutral.com

TreeNeutral

Printed in the United States of America on acid-free paper

19 20 21 22 23 24   10 9 8 7 6 5 4 3 2 1

First Edition

DEDICATED TO THE
TEACHERS, COACHES, AND BOSSES IN OUR LIVES
WHO HELPED SHAPE THIS BOOK.

The constant facade of order hides the wilderness that is craving to seep out and teach us that life wasn't created to be what we think it is. Beyond words, we must experience the wilderness to be taught what cannot be otherwise known.

—DR. SERENE JONES

Contents

Preface

MITCH WAS OUR NATIONAL director of sales and my boss. I worked under him in my new role as sales manager of the western district for a medical equipment company. He was smart, tough, stubborn, impatient, and demanding. He also had other annoying qualities. He constantly pushed, prodded, and challenged most everything I did. Mitch did not create what I would call a comfortable work environment for me, nor would I consider him an easygoing manager.

He took a keen interest in my development from the get-go, and I remember wishing he hadn't been quite so invested in my performance as a first-time manager. I felt he expected more from me than from the other managers and was more critical of my work, which made me want to avoid him at times. While he never told me what to do, he constantly questioned my actions and decisions. He forced me to painstakingly analyze every option and consider every detail. There was always a lesson to be learned. He taught me to evaluate how my actions would affect our business, our employees, and our clients. I'd just come from a sales-producer role, so this was not how I was accustomed to thinking. Looking back, I see that nothing ever came easy while working for him.

Mitch made sure I took full responsibility for what happened in the region I managed, including what my salespeople did and did not do. And excuses were not acceptable. He gave me the proverbial kick in the rear when needed and complimented me when appropriate. There was an overriding code that was unspoken yet obvious to those who were part of his team: maximum effort and results were not optional. This high-performance environment created a feeling of what I now call *healthy discomfort*; the discomfort wasn't fear-based, but an emotion more like what I felt before a big exam or athletic competition.

Speaking of exams, it was not uncommon for Mitch to give us a written pop quiz on the technicalities of a new product or single us out during a meeting with a challenging question. When in his presence during the workday, discussions about sales performance and new strategies were inevitable and would often turn heated. It used to frustrate me because I knew, whether he agreed with my thought or strategy or not, he would take the opposite position just to challenge my thinking.

What I adored about Mitch's management style was his belief that if a person never failed, they weren't trying hard enough. So I took great liberties in this area. Begging for forgiveness versus asking permission was my mantra, and Mitch let me know he tolerated my missteps because he saw an early version of himself in my behaviors. Working for him came with an odd mix of emotions: I was never fearful of losing my job, I was always provided continuing-education opportunities, vacation time was never tracked or discussed, and my expenses and travel were never challenged by him, but there was *always* tension in the air created by his demands for perpetual growth.

Mitch openly communicated that he saw great potential in me as a leader and would push me to achieve that potential. His actions and behaviors let me know I wasn't just some asset or tool that allowed him to hit the sales goal. He cared about me as a person. He often invited me to personal dinners at his house, and we would have poignant conversations about family and raising kids. He even made sure our wives spent time together.

Despite all this, Mitch has the distinction of being the most challenging and frustrating person to whom I've ever reported. But he has also been the greatest growth catalyst in my professional career. Only now can I look back with enough clarity to understand what Mitch was trying to do and his reasons for it. Simply stated, Mitch cared enough to make me uncomfortable. And although he never said it, he seemed to intuitively understand that being in a state of discomfort is the only way a person can grow.

Sadly, the "Mitches" of the world are the exception and not the rule in leadership and coaching roles. If you doubt me, take a moment and consider all the teachers, coaches, and bosses you've had in your life to date. Could you list fifty? One hundred? Perhaps two hundred? Now think about *only* those that had such a positive impact on your life that you might say, "I wouldn't be where I am today without that person in my life." Could you say that about two people? Three? Maybe five? I have done this exercise with thousands of leaders across the globe, and it is rare that anyone says they had more of these influencers than they can show on one hand. That is a sad reality check about a role that, at its core, is designed to elevate you to levels you could not otherwise achieve.

High-performing teams and their coaches have always been fascinating to me. In my early years, I was captivated by Vince Lombardi and the Green Bay Packers, John Wooden and UCLA, and Tom Osborne and Husker football. As I matured, this interest evolved to include people like Lee Iacocca with Chrysler and Lou Gerstner with IBM. Why do some teams always achieve while others wallow in mediocrity? Early on, I knew it had to be because they had strong leaders. *First, Break All the Rules*, a best-selling leadership book released in the late nineties, fueled my curiosity with its research and affirmed my beliefs. This book showed it was the manager that made all the difference.

I did not begin my career with the goal of getting into management. The first ten years were spent in commissioned sales, and while successful in that arena, I always found myself gravitating toward helping others sell. Though I couldn't articulate why at the time, there was something more innately satisfying to me about motivating others to achieve. Since that first management job working under Mitch, I've worked only in leadership roles, tackling everything from regional sales management to an executive position with a publicly traded company. I've experienced a variety of bosses, some life changing in the way they coached and others who were just bad, but I've learned from them all. Personally, as a coach I've been far from perfect, but I would like to think I've touched lives and businesses in a way more positive than not.

When I was promoted to my first leadership role, I had eight salespeople reporting to me, but besides Mitch I found no resources and tools to help me learn what to do as a leader. There were thousands of books I could have given to my salespeople to help them improve their skills, but there was nothing that defined, taught, and quantified my role, which I viewed as identical to that of a coach. So I worked to hone my skills in a variety of ways, many of which took me outside of sales. I learned from and engaged with sports psychologists. I studied the latest leadership models. I got to know and quizzed PhDs in organization behavior. I conducted my own research, and had my own good old-fashioned experiences. Eventually, I reached a point in my career where I realized I should take what I had learned about being a successful leader and share it with others. I knew I could be that resource that the field of management was missing.

In 2008, I started EcSell Institute, a company whose vision is to *create a workplace where every employee knows what great coaching feels like.* My plan was and still is to accomplish this by working only with department leaders, with most of EcSell's work focusing on sales leadership. The other strategic caveats were that all EcSell programs would be created and supported with research, and success would only be measured by correlating coaching activities and behaviors to revenue and performance growth. The motivation for starting EcSell Institute came about for two reasons: (1) my passion for understanding the science behind a leader's impact on performance and growth and (2) my termination from my last executive role. I'd be lying if I said getting fired wasn't devastating at the time, but for reasons you will learn later, that humbling day had a profound impact on the trajectory of my life and the lives of those around me.

The early years at EcSell were more discomforting and costlier than I ever imagined. Our small team worked hard to create and sell something nobody had ever sold—a measurable coaching methodology, the outcome of which quantifies effectiveness of those in leadership roles. On several occasions, I thought we would fold, but our committed team always made something happen when necessary to keep us alive.

At the risk of braggadocio, my greatest coaching strength is identifying and acquiring highly talented people. And these people, who now compose the EcSell team, continually amaze not just me and our clients but also one another. While I receive a great deal of the accolades (I have been featured on the cover of magazines and in newspaper articles; I did a TEDx Talk that went viral; and I have been asked to do countless podcasts, radio shows, workshops, and speeches across the globe), none of this would have happened without the talent, passion, and work of our team. It is easy to be humble when you realize your success is because of others.

Nothing elevates performance more than coaching has been our consistent why, and it guides our research, service, sales, and strategy. Technology and research have substantially changed what work we deliver and how we deliver it, but nothing has influenced our delivery model more than my brilliant colleague and coauthor, Sarah Wirth.

Many pages of this book are dedicated to explaining how discomfort and challenge are necessary to achieve growth of any kind—personal growth, professional growth, and revenue growth. Sarah certainly acts as a comfort disrupter for me and our business. I often describe her as the yin to my yang because, even though we are different in many ways, we complement each other with our abilities. I tend to lead with ideas, data, emotions, and passion. Sarah views everything with logic—how what we're offering can be applied. I get excited about how we can affect people by helping them become better coaches; Sarah likes to analyze the impact of coaching on the bottom line. But we are aligned in our belief, based on both emotion and logic, that growth only occurs in a state of discomfort, and leaders at every level have the greatest impact on the discomfort levels of their teams.

Sarah has spent her career studying the impact of great leadership. She graduated from Michigan Law School but knew the legal profession wasn't the right fit for her. So rather than taking a lucrative job offer at a national law firm, she decided to work for an employee selection and development company. She spent the next decade studying the talents of leaders at world-renowned organizations like The Cheesecake Factory, the Ritz-Carlton Hotel Company, and the Estée Lauder Companies. Doing this work was where her love of analyzing the impact of effective coaching on a company's bottom line was born.

In the years since, Sarah has developed a knack for figuring out the right questions to ask to understand how leaders create growth. Turning research data into insights, her special talent is distilling complex ideas into simple concepts to share with others. Sarah was raised by two teachers, so her drive to learn, ask questions, and help others discover new ways of working comes naturally to her. She may be logical and love data, but you truly see her come alive when she's sharing what she's learned with others. When I recruited Sarah to join EcSell Institute seven years ago, I was looking for someone who could help take our company to the next level in client service. We were doing a good job of growing and acquiring new customers, but I knew we needed to be offering more if we were going to retain them. Sarah agreed to join our team and ultimately developed the client-service model that would deepen our research into the connection between coaching and measurable growth.

Since our company's inception, we have studied more than one hundred thousand coaching interactions to understand the behaviors and activities of what we now refer to as *high-growth coaches*. What we've learned is that coaches who drive significant growth operate differently than their peers. They are more consistent and accountable in their actions. They are better at developing trusting relationships with the people they lead. And most importantly, they do not worry about creating discomfort because they know they must challenge their team and make them uncomfortable in order to help them grow.

In this book, you will hear a combined voice—mine and Sarah's—so *we* will be primarily used as opposed to *I* in our writing. Also, the book includes real-life examples and stories of coaching successes that come from our experiences from within as well as outside the world of business.

The book is *written to* executive leaders within every company, because ultimately you own the performance environment of the entire organization. Growth and resulting revenue are being unnecessarily left on the table by every business we have researched, and this should shake you to the core. But this book is *written for* frontline managers who must become the catalyst for their team's growth. And, despite my sales background, this applies to everyone who has a team reporting to them. A team of any kind reflects how it is coached, and growth will not be maximized unless the manager drives it.

Continue reading and you will learn about the tools, processes, behaviors, and best practices that high-growth coaches use to create high-performing teams. You will be introduced to a step-by-step coaching methodology that is proven to increase results. You will understand the importance of measuring the effectiveness of coaching as well as how to accurately assess coaching *quantity* and coaching *quality*, and how they affect revenue.

Finally, this book is based on research and best practices, *not opinion*! You will see how our research is used to draw conclusions as well as detailed case studies of how the proper amount of coaching activities and high-quality coaching creates growth and improved performance. When you finish this book, you will know exactly what managers need to do to become high-growth coaches. Most importantly, if we were to interview your team for a sequel to this book, we hope they would tell us how *you* evolved from being just a "comfortable manager" to the greatest growth catalyst for your team's professional career, just like Mitch was for me.

Acknowledgments

THIS IS THE SECTION of the book that is typically read by only close friends, family, or those who want to know if their name is mentioned. For those who do not fall into the aforementioned categories, you may feel comfortable skipping these next few paragraphs, and you should. But before you fast-forward to the introduction, let us first challenge you to walk through an exercise related to this section: If you were to write a book about your life, who would you list in the acknowledgments section? Make that list and either call or send a note to those who positively coached and mentored you, thanking them for the investment. Doing so will touch their lives and make them smile. We could certainly use more of that in our world.

Regardless of how many of these books sell, we consider writing this book a great accomplishment. We have spent countless hours on this project and have temporarily diverted attention away from those we love, those with whom we work, and those for whom we work. But, as with most great accomplishments, there is an invaluable team of people without whom this book would not have advanced. At EcSell Institute we get an incredible amount of work done with a few people because those few people are extremely talented and efficient. They are peak performers and are infinitely fun (and challenging) to coach. In no particular order, the balance of our leadership team consists of:

Kerstin Eckstrom, former COO and the much better half of the last name we share. Most anyone would have thought I was crazy to start a business during the Great Recession, but she believed in my idea and in me even more, which says a lot since I had just lost my job. In our new business, she made sure every bill got paid and every form got filed. She fulfilled every task and duty that nobody else would step up to do, with amazing class. She allowed our family room to become a conference room and gave keys to our now "home/office" to several people, trusting that they would use them wisely. Twenty years of daily order and family privacy were thrown out the window as she acquiesced to finding people wandering around our home with their laptops in hand and likely engaging in phone conversations about the behaviors of effective leaders. She is the humblest, most patient, and most giving woman I know, and I am lucky to call her my wife.

Will Kloefkorn, VP of sales. The first person I hired needed to sell, and Will certainly does that. He leads with his heart, has been unwavering in his commitment to our success, and is arguably the most passionate person regarding the impact of coaching on performance. He is wise beyond his years and, while he has an old soul, he is childlike (not childish) in his approach to most everything. It is not uncommon to find Will standing in the "kids" buffet line at a wedding dinner. Most adults would never think of such a thing, even though mac and cheese and corn dogs sound better than a piece of dry beef with mixed veggies.

Stacia Jorgensen, director of research. What a rare find. She not only has a background in research but also in sociology. She is more brilliant and creative than she would admit (so we remind her frequently), which is evidenced by her ability to develop solutions to any research problem we encounter. She works in a humble, servant manner, and our entire team becomes giddy anytime we receive an email from her that begins with "I have been fooling around with our data and found something interesting . . ."

Kathy Collins, VP of operations. Easily the surrogate mother to us all and the most organized person with whom I've ever worked. Our coaching cloud software would not be operational were it not for her unparalleled thoroughness (she ranks in the 96th percentile in thoroughness, and she will forever be searching for the 4 percent that somehow slipped her grasp), and she goes to extreme lengths to make sure every client is happy with our work. She always leads with love, and we do our best to emulate what she brings to our collective table. Kathy has the rare ability to work with extreme urgency but never misses dotting an *i* or crossing a *t*, and the entire team implicitly trusts this amazing human.

Anna Schott, director of marketing. For someone who claims to have been a timid soul from small-town Nebraska, she sure has learned to take the bull by the horns. She is one of the braver people I've met and has more moxie than most individuals should be allowed to have. She went from a college intern role to leading our marketing the day after her graduation, and if you are wondering how the marketing world looks through young eyes, it is much more refreshing than the view from my seasoned lenses.

Claire Eckstrom, director of public relations and events. Yes, my daughter. The most recent addition to our team, she brings a unique set of gifts to the business-development side of our organization. Spending years in the fashion business and living in New York City, she has developed a professional edge that allows her to get stuff done. She is fearless, wicked smart, calm under pressure, engaging, and vivacious, and she loves working in complex environments. I try to be as objective as possible regarding her strengths, but those are all words our team has used.

Beyond our EcSell team, we have been fortunate to have a number of personal and professional mentors throughout our lives who have affected us profoundly and helped us understand what it feels like to have a great coach. There are also family and friends who contributed in other ways, and we wish to acknowledge those people. Understanding how Complexity works (and you are about to), if any one of those listed in the following paragraphs had not been a part of our lives, it is likely nobody would be reading this book. In no particular order:

Bill's significant influencers: Dad and Mom, who always believed in me and would say, "Why not you?"; my wife, Kerstin, and my amazing children, Will, Claire, and Maddie, you make me feel like I hung the moon; my brothers and sisters, Greg, Karen, Mark, Mikal, and Tom, you make me feel loved; my in-laws, Tom and Cynthia; my cousins, you know who you are; our dog, Aspen, who loves unconditionally; my surrogate parents, Bob and Carolyn; my friends Tom, Brad, Karen, and Dr. Mary; my teachers Mrs.

Bell and Mr. Yahnke; my coaches John and Ed; and my discomfort-creating boss, Bill (a.k.a. Mitch).

Sarah's significant influencers: Mom and Dad, for their belief in me; Nick, for always challenging me; Miles and Emmett, for teaching me about unconditional love; Sasha, for always listening and never judging; Malcolm, Amy, and Angie, for showing me what true leadership looks like; Coach Johnson and Mr. Altig, for introducing me to the impact of a great coach; and most of all, Mike, for demonstrating every day what it means to love, support, push, and invest in the people most important to you. You are truly the best coach I've ever known.

Introduction

IT IS 8:30 A.M. in southern Florida and the summer humidity is already oppressive, but the young athletes are moving with precision around the clay court as if programmed by the latest sports video game. They have been working since 7:00 a.m.; a few began at 6:30. Rene is barking encouragement and instruction, and though his Spanish accent makes it challenging for me to understand, it is infinitely clear that the students know what he wants.

There is little time for rest; the renowned coach's intensity does not allow for complacency. The kids move station to station, drill to drill, with brief breaks to mop off sweat, quickly change their shirts, and guzzle water. Working hard is not an option; the players self-select in or out of his culture. If the kids are not playing with heart and soul, they are asked to sit or go home, and "home" means for good. The unwritten rule regarding an injury is that if you are injured, you do not play. If you play, you are not injured. Most every aspect of their tennis game is worked on daily. There are approximately twenty players, and each is called by their given name.

Rene Gomez has coached the likes of Andre Agassi, Jim Courier, Anna Kournikova, and Monica Seles, so he knows what it takes to play tennis at the highest level. He doesn't talk to the kids about playing professionally; they only discuss disciplines and act in ways that take their game up one notch at a time, one day at a time. And when the next rung on the ladder is reached, the coach turns up the heat once again—more conditioning, more strokes, and more mental resolve. For many of the teenagers here, according to Rene, the only difference between them and Maria Sharapova is toughness, both mental and physical.

Beyond Rene, the most important pieces to the high-performance puzzle at Gomez Tennis Academy are his assistant coaches. Rene works with all his students, but it is not physically possible for a single person to provide the needed attention, so it's up to his assistant coaches to grow and develop all the talent. The assistants are the ones pointing out specific tweaks a player can make to their swing. They're the ones offering words of praise and encouragement to someone who is working hard. They're the ones barking challenges to someone who needs to step up their game. They're the ones counseling a homesick teenager. Every day, all day, they're the ones on the front lines, demanding extreme effort from their players so that they can reach their full performance potential. While the culture begins at the top, without the other coaches supporting the vision and executing high-growth activities, the program would fail.

THIS STORY IS AN example of high-growth coaches working in a demanding, high-performance environment. The players are there to grow, to separate themselves from the pack, to see how far they can take their game, to test themselves every day. And because they are not there to be ordinary but rather exceptional, their coaches cannot be ordinary. Coaches must perpetuate, not cap growth; their actions and behaviors must drive performance improvement in a healthy way. Likewise, this book is not about being ordinary; it's about achieving excellence and helping others achieve results they would not attain without a high-growth coach in their life.

COACHES ARE THE KEY TO PERFORMANCE AND GROWTH

These high-performance environments allow you to measure inputs and outcomes at every level, from how well the players play to how well the coaches coach, and these measurements can then be used as a baseline for growth. In a high-performance environment, those team members not willing to continually improve or to push or be pushed will not find a home.

These types of organizations, whether a youth tennis academy or a Fortune 500 company, know how to identify and acquire high-performing talent, but just as importantly they know how to develop and retain talent. To a high-performing business, developing talent is the essential function of their managers, rather than just one of their priorities. Managers and their team members have used the term *healthy tension* to describe how high-performance environments feel. They push

> EVERY GROWTH CHALLENGE A BUSINESS FACES IS A MANAGEMENT ISSUE.

themselves and their teams to constantly improve, and being "too busy" is never an excuse for not getting done what is most important. The success of high-performance teams depends on their coaches.

At EcSell, we learned long ago that every growth challenge a business faces is a management issue. How often have we seen the same team perform at an entirely different level depending on their leader? The examples in the sports world are endless, and you can probably point to an example or two in your own professional experience. Great coaches have such a positive effect on their team's performance because they believe every aspect of growth is their responsibility, and they behave accordingly. Think about it: from hiring talent to player development, planning, strategy, accountability, and motivation, coaches affect everything.

DISCRETIONARY EFFORT: YOUR COACHING VALUE

To understand the value you bring to your team as their coach, ask yourself the following question: Will people on your team still do their job without you as their manager? For example, when a sales manager goes on vacation, will the salespeople who work under him or her still show up for work and continue to sell? Leaders of all levels in organizations—and we've asked more than a thousand—answer that yes, of course their teams do work without them being physically present. So, if your people can still do their jobs without you, the value you bring to them and the organization is measured by how much better they will do their jobs with you as their manager. If you manage a sales team, your value equals how much more your team sells because of you.

The additional amount produced by a team, measured in dollars, productivity, wins, and so on, *because of a manager* is what we refer to as *discretionary effort*. It's how much more work gets done, how much a team's efficiency increases, how much a team's quality improves, or how much more is sold because of a manager. If a sales team would produce $10 million without a manager and they sell $14 million with one, the $4 million difference is the monetary value of the discretionary effort obtained by the manager. With the right tools and data, any organization can now measure the discretionary effort managers bring to their teams (more on this later).

> THERE IS A CORRELATION BETWEEN HIGH-PERFORMING TEAMS AND MANAGERS WHO CREATE HEALTHY DISCOMFORT FOR THOSE ON THEIR TEAM.

Part of what we have found through our research and will show in this book is how managers create discretionary effort over long periods of time. It is important to note that discretionary effort should not just be measured at a single point in time. For example, in business, a manager who uses fear as a motivator can get discretionary effort for short periods of time, but it is not likely to be sustainable. Though fear can create growth, it is not a healthy way to achieve it, and over time fear will likely lead to a low-growth, chaotic environment. That said, we did find in our research (which we will show later) that there is a correlation between high-performing teams and managers who create healthy discomfort for those on their team.

Some team members describe their managers as nice and feel their managers have created a comfortable team environment in which to work. Just to be clear, we're not saying there's anything wrong with managers being nice or creating some feeling of comfort. But nice managers don't obtain nearly as much discretionary effort as high-growth coaches who create discomfort. If a manager is simply nice, they're not creating the healthy tension, the discomfort, that leads to optimum performance. They're not pushing their team members outside their comfort zones to get them to grow. And they're certainly not creating a performance environment like the ones we see with a great sports team or a high-growth company. But how do we measure a manager's ability to create this type of environment?

MANAGERIAL EFFECTIVENESS MUST BE MEASURED

Data that measures employee effectiveness is by no means new, especially in sales, where many companies track most every selling activity imaginable through tools such as customer relationship management (CRM) systems. However, consider the following exchange and think if it applies to your company.

A while back, we had a conversation with a VP of sales who had a litany of frontline sales managers reporting to him. Not everyone on his teams was achieving their sales goals, and he was searching for answers. When we asked what data they regularly reviewed, he shared all the metrics they track, showing virtually every minute of how a salesperson spent their day. They measured the number of sales calls made, where they traveled, customers or prospects called, ratio of deals closed, and so on. They had an endless stream of data on what their salespeople did. But when asked what his managers were doing to drive growth, he said, "Guys, I understand why you are asking and want you to know I've been working with most of my managers for more than ten years, so I trust them all. They are not only work colleagues; they are good friends. But having said that, I have no idea where they were last week, let alone last month. Plus, I have no idea if they are doing the activities or behaving in a way that drives the most growth because I have no idea what those things are. I guess I've just always hoped my managers were doing the right things."

The attitude in this frustrating exchange is unfortunately commonplace in every work environment we've researched. For the heads of organizations to know nothing about the activities, behaviors, and overall effectiveness of the role that has the greatest impact on team performance, the manager, is ludicrous. Common sense dictates that nobody comes to work with a goal of failing, but the manager's role is arguably the most precarious regarding longevity. We see firsthand how companies are quick to release managers, and a revolving door is set in motion, especially in sales departments. A big reason for this chaotic turnover is that nobody helps them understand how to be effective, nor is anyone measuring their performance inputs or outcomes. Time and again, we speak with senior executives who have no idea how their managers are spending their days or even how they should be spending them. Even managers themselves question if they're focused on the activities that produce the best team results.

To sustain growth, maximize the performance of your business and teams, attract the best talent, and ensure that your organization remains relevant in today's and especially tomorrow's workplace, resources must be committed to the continual development and quantification of managerial effectiveness. The goal of this commitment, and hopefully an outcome of reading this book, is to get managers to behave and drive results in a way that resembles a *high-growth coach* as opposed to a performance-limiting manager.

You've probably noticed by now that we prefer the word *coach* to *manager*. That's for a very specific reason: the term *manager* is an archaic term describing a role that, by definition, limits growth and performance. A manager oversees managing tasks and managing people to accomplish those tasks. They promote processes and order, but those are not the elements that lead to growth. On the other hand, a coach develops and inspires people to do their best work. Coaches obtain more discretionary effort than managers, which is why the best coaches elevate their team's performance.

MANAGER IS AN ARCHAIC TERM DESCRIBING A ROLE THAT, BY DEFINITION, LIMITS GROWTH AND PERFORMANCE.

For many people, the word *coach* triggers association with athletic teams, for which the job description is simple: to win. Indeed, the role of coaching in athletics encompasses the same key elements as effectively leading a business team. The coach must manage processes and outputs, develop relationships, lead and inspire, strategize, recruit, and certainly create discomfort for their team to achieve maximum performance. In addition to *coach* being more robust than previous descriptors of the manager, the title and role of a coach (which is detailed in chapter 2) more clearly defines what is required in business to consistently grow. Going forward, we will primarily use the word *coach* as opposed to *manager*.

Even if we know that the word *coach* and related coaching activities better describe what it takes to lead a high-growth team, there is still a significant lack of understanding of what a coach needs to do in a business environment to be successful. In our research with sales departments, we see that approximately 80 percent of existing coaches, even those who've had coaching training, are not executing the necessary coaching activities with the right frequency or quality that will lead a team to perform at the highest levels (we'll discuss why in future chapters). We also see that 30 percent of the coaches in a sales department are either providing no discretionary effort or unknowingly preventing salespeople from selling more. Said another way, sales departments are paying, on average, 30 percent of their coaches to inhibit sales.

> SALES DEPARTMENTS ARE PAYING, ON AVERAGE,
> 30 PERCENT OF THEIR COACHES TO INHIBIT SALES.

When we set out on our journey to understand and quantify how coaches influence growth and overall performance, our vision was to discern the activities, behaviors, and tools the best coaches use. We deliberately began our work in sales departments for several reasons, one being the background of those on the EcSell team. Another reason was that sales departments traditionally do a better job tracking performance data. Having such black-and-white numbers (every business tracks sales) made it easier for us to correlate coaching activities and behaviors to results.

The more we learned about how coaches affect sales results and as we shared these findings with CEOs, presidents, and other executives throughout the world, they would in turn share their belief that effective coaching in the sales world should apply to every department. While we always believed this as well, their response motivated us to expand our work to almost every type of leader and team in an organization. However, you will see that most of the examples in the following chapters use sales departments because we have so much rich data.

WHAT MAKES AN EFFECTIVE COACH?

We had many discoveries along the way as we sought to understand what made certain coaches more effective than others. These discoveries are the foundation of the coaching methods and best practices that we share in the coming chapters, but here are a few of our most exciting insights:

- We discovered that high-growth coaches perform specific activities whose effectiveness and execution can be measured. This insight was our most important initial discovery because it showed us that we could quantify what the best coaches did differently. And if we could identify and measure coaching activities, then we could also educate other coaches on what to do to increase their own effectiveness.

- We discovered that high-growth coaches not only have specific coaching activities they perform regularly but also exhibit unique behaviors when coaching. A huge part of our research has come through surveying employees about their coaches. As we saw how employees rated their coaches on dozens of different behaviors, it became obvious that high-growth coaches simply coach in a different way.

- We discovered that these successful coaching activities and behaviors could be quantified, taught, and implemented by those willing to change. As we measured coaches over time, many over the course of years, we often saw significant changes in their activities and behaviors. Coaches who focused on improving the quality and quantity of their coaching in turn had team members who gave them higher marks in their overall coaching acumen. And, not surprisingly, the coaches' measurable performance improved. For sales coaches, it meant their teams sold more.

In spite of our excitement at all of these discoveries, one discovery we made was more significant than all the others—the discomfort factor. Just like my manager Mitch or tennis coach Rene Gomez, high-growth coaches are not afraid to push, to demand, and to challenge to get their teams to perform. They don't shy away from making their team members uncomfortable. In fact, they relish it because they consciously or subconsciously know that growth can only occur in a state of discomfort. Their goal is to get the best possible performance out of the people they coach, and they must move beyond just being a nice manager to make it happen.

Perhaps the reason the discomfort factor was so significant is because it really surprised us. We had been measuring and quantifying coaching behavior for a while, but there seemed to be a concept we were missing. And it wasn't until we worked with a brilliant university professor, Dr. Mary Uhl-Bien, that we discovered what it was: the best coaches embrace or create an environment of discomfort to get those on their team to grow.

Our journey of discovery will not end as long as there is more to learn about great coaching. While we have our own opinions and ideas about coaching, it is our goal to always let the data guide us. So, as you continue reading, know that everything we are sharing with you is based on our research, which includes the following:

- **Objectively measuring more than one hundred thousand coaching interactions in the workplace.** This was primarily executed through a coaching cloud software that we developed for the single purpose of quantifying and understanding coaching effectiveness within an organization. The software allows our clients to cut and slice coaching data in a variety of ways, examples of which will be shown throughout the following chapters.

- **Surveying more than seven thousand employees and managers in various roles and companies throughout the world.** Surveys were used to discover and dissect the relationship between employees and their coaches. We call this our *Through the Eyes of the Team* survey, and you will see many of our survey findings throughout the book. This data comes directly from the individuals who experience the interactions with their coach.

- **Working directly with our own clients.** We interact daily with executives and coaches throughout the world. We listen to their challenges, needs, and ideas about coaching, which keeps us attuned to what is happening at every leadership level in an organization.

- **Conducting focus groups of executives, managers, and employees.** We have met face-to-face and over the phone with groups throughout the world at all different levels, in all different markets, that encompass everything from agriculture to high-tech to health care to learn their perceptions of great coaching. The ideas and concepts they share continue to shape and inform our formal research efforts.

As you read this book, know that coaching is hard and, candidly, most managers don't do what it takes to be categorized as *high-growth coaches*. When we refer to a high-growth coach, we are referring to coaches of teams that are producing in the top 20 percent of their coaching peers within the same company. For example, in a sales department that has a team of one hundred coaches, while we research them all, we separate the twenty highest-performing coaches measured by their team percent to goal. We then look for differences in coaching activity and behavior. The same goes for a company that has ten coaches; we study them all but look for what is different about the top two.

When the top 20 percent are analyzed, these facts emerge:

- They do 30 percent more coaching activities than the bottom 80 percent.

- They coach with 18 percent better quality than the bottom 80 percent.

- They coach teams that average 110 percent of goal, while the bottom 80 percent average 91 percent.

- They coach teams that produce an average of $4.1 million more sales revenue than the bottom 80 percent.

Using our data, if a sales department has fifty frontline managers, they can safely assume that forty of them, due to poor coaching, are leaving a combined $164 million in revenue on the table. Those figures should cause every leader to stop in their tracks and want to know more about what their coaches are doing and how well they are doing it.

We will analyze, in detail, the science of performance and growth and how coaches perpetuate or limit the performance or growth of individuals and teams. We will share the specifics of who we research, how we research, and what benchmarks apply to everyone in a coaching role. There will then be a series of chapters that detail measurable and quantifiable coaching activities and behaviors that we have proven lead to improved performance and sustained team growth.

Most of the book justifiably focuses on what coaches can do to drive more performance from individuals and teams, but the concluding chapter details how an organization can adopt and implement coaching best practices. We will share a four-step coaching methodology that can be utilized by businesses of all sizes to create a team of high-growth coaches, the outcome of which measures and quantifies coaching activities, behaviors, and overall coaching effectiveness.

Throughout this book, we share business case studies that outline how differing companies transformed their management team. You will read how their committed journey to high-growth coaching affected sales results, but you will also be aware of the pain they incurred doing so. We will candidly share the realities that occur when behaviors are asked to change—managers who don't want their work (or lack thereof) exposed, managers who are comfortable with how they work and don't want to be accountable for a new way of coaching, managers who say they don't have time, and managers who don't want their work quantified. But you will also read about managers who do adapt and then adopt a high-growth coaching methodology and how their team outcomes look and feel different. You will hear from team members who have poor coaches and those who have high-growth coaches. And, because we always correlate coaching to performance and growth, you will see the good, bad, and ugly data of a variety of coaches who lead sales teams.

While the results that high-growth coaches achieve are likely to sound attractive to you, and they should, it is challenging to consistently execute what a high-growth coach does without a strong personal desire or organizational commitment to learn, grow, and change. Our research clearly shows that what we are espousing is different than what most managers do today, which therefore creates discomfort and organizational disruption. However, because of our research, we have learned to embrace discomfort, and by the time you are finished with this book, we hope you will too. Because being in a state of discomfort is the only way to continually grow.

Finally, before we get started, I'd like to propose an important question.

WHAT DOES IT FEEL LIKE TO BE COACHED BY YOU?

This is a succinct, simple question that should evoke great thought. Whether you are a frontline manager or executive leader, I encourage you to challenge yourself by answering it. Before you read further, stop and write down the question and your answer. Do it now on the lines that follow.

_____

_____

_____

In EcSell's coaching academies with leaders from across the world, we most often begin by asking this question. Although the responses obviously vary, what remains the same is that most of these leaders have never even considered this question, nor do they have an analytical understanding of how effective they are at improving individual and team performance.

Not knowing how your team feels about your coaching effectiveness is unacceptable. The managers and executive leaders within any organization are the obstacles, catalysts, decision makers, and solutions for growth. The challenge in having empirical data about your coaching effectiveness is that you are not only exposed but you are also holding a mirror up to yourself, which is hard for most everyone. It is tough to see a reality in which those on your team may not believe you care about them beyond the workplace or in which you are not at your best when under pressure or in which you inhibit the growth of those on your team.

Discovering this may create discomfort, but it also creates an amazing growth opportunity. Naïveté is no longer an excuse for not having a data-driven understanding of what it feels like to be coached by you.

1

The Growth Rings

Question: What does your manager do best as a sales coach?
Answer: I don't know. I've never been coached.

—Through the Eyes of the Team survey respondent

IN THE EARLY YEARS of our company, our small EcSell team spent countless hours in coffee shops, restaurants, our family room (before we could afford an office), or any place that would allow our patronage while we obsessively debated and analyzed how coaches contributed to high-performing teams. We knew that coaching had the most significant impact on performance. We knew there was something to high-growth coaching that classic leadership and management models were not explaining. But figuring out how to research and explain it had us stumped.

We assumed coaches understood that their primary role was to create growth above and beyond what their subordinates were willing to do on their own, but our work with clients proved we were wrong. So to help managers better comprehend what to do and how to do it well, we studied basic coaching activities and behaviors. However, the more we researched, the more we learned that the best leaders were unique in their coaching, and we could see that—either intentionally or unintentionally—they created or embraced an environment of discomfort as a growth mechanism. But why did these behaviors have such powerful outcomes? What was it about discomfort that created so much growth?

Ironically, it all came together when we injected some discomfort into our own discussions by inviting leadership guru Mary Uhl-Bien, PhD, to work with us. Her research background, profound knowledge, and passion for the study of leadership helped us view growth through a different lens. She constantly challenged and expanded our myopic views on the role of a coach-leader versus a manager.

Dr. Mary was invaluable in assisting with a paramount discovery that was quite literally an epiphany, a "holy $#it" moment that stopped us in our tracks. What began as a journey to understand how coaching affects the performance of individuals and teams had turned into a global model for explaining how growth is sustained and amplified by *all* living things. We discovered a model that showed *why* exponential and sustained growth only occur in a state of discomfort. We call this model the *Growth Rings*.

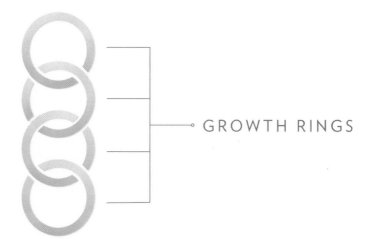

GROWTH RINGS

Since this discovery, we have spent years on additional research, challenging the concept, refining it, and finding understandable ways to explain it. And after communicating the Growth Rings to more than a thousand presidents, CEOs, and various executives; another eighteen hundred people at the University of Nevada TEDx event; and an astonishing two million (and growing) who have since viewed the "Why Comfort Will Ruin Your Life"[1] TEDx Talk online, we know the Growth Rings are resonating with business leaders and have immense performance applications to all businesses throughout the world. Even more, since the TEDx Talk introduced the Growth Rings, our company has been inundated with emails, tweets, Facebook posts, phone calls, and LinkedIn messages from people around the world with professional and personal stories of how the Growth Rings have already affected them as well as those on their teams.

For us, understanding the Growth Rings has changed how we parent, coach, view adversity, and think about human behavior. The Growth Rings have altered how we view the world and thrive within differing environments (or opt out of them). The Growth Rings have played a powerful role in our personal peace and emotional development.

The Growth Rings illustrate differing environments that exist in our world and how they either promote or hinder growth. Each ring encompasses one of four primary environments: Stagnation, Order, Complexity, and Chaos.

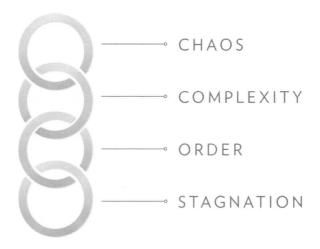

1   Bill Eckstrom, "TEDx Talk: Why Comfort Will Ruin Your Life," February 7, 2017, TEDxUniversityofNevada Talk, https://www.ecsellinstitute.com/sales-coaching-blog/tedx-talk-why-comfort-will-ruin-your-life-transcript.

These primary environments could represent one's dorm room, home, place of work, government, sports team, nature, and especially one's body and mind. The growth state of every living thing can be represented within a Growth Ring. And, while we'll explain all the environments that compose the Growth Rings in detail, we will take a more expansive look into Order and Complexity. Order and Complexity are the environments that are most represented in high-growth teams and therefore more applicable to coaching and growth.

Stagnation

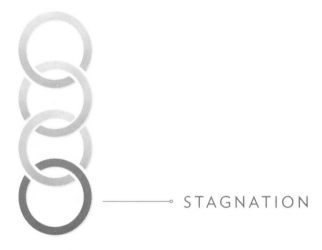

The first Growth Ring represents a low-performing, low, or negative growth environment called *Stagnation*. Stagnation is a situation in which people may need to follow too many steps, get someone else's permission, or deal with minutia that stifle creativity, independent thought, or action. Stagnation isn't a popular or common environment, but it exists in certain businesses, homes, and natural places. Stagnated environments don't just freeze growth; they regress it. Stagnation causes environments within nature to wither and die (think about old, rotting forests and stagnant water); it causes our bodies to lose muscle and our minds to lose imagination.

By the time a business reaches Stagnation, drastic measures need to be taken to reverse the decline. These may include, but are not limited to, changes in leadership personnel, rapid evolutions in products and services and how they are marketed, adjustments in markets, the hiring of outside consultants, and so on. Surprisingly, we have worked with very few businesses in this environmental ring, perhaps for the very same reasons they are in Stagnation—they are not willing to change. Although more examples abound, the most common example of a stagnated environment is a local or federal government bureaucracy. In these cultures, performance improvement, creativity, effective collaboration, and working out of the norm are not highly valued. They are all components of high-growth teams.

Chaos

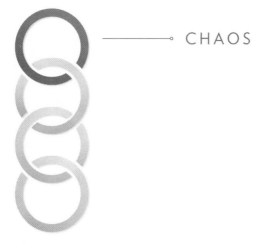

CHAOS

The antithesis of Stagnation is an environment called *Chaos*. Also low-growth and low-performance, Chaos can be caused by internal or external events or conditions. Chaos may be a temporary state that occurs (for example, in the early stages of a new business). We also see Chaos ensue as the result of natural disasters and horrific events like 9/11 and, though less tragic, business mergers and acquisitions.

We have often visited with leaders and employees from newly acquired companies that have no idea to whom they report, how their duties are affected, or if their employment will be retained. Behaviors exhibited in chaotic environments typify those when fear is present; fear tends to trigger in our brains one of the three *F*s: freeze, fight, or flight.

A graphic example occurred recently with an acquired company in the Midwest. We received several calls from longtime employees of the acquired company who were devastated over the outcome of the acquisition. They didn't believe that strategic direction commitments by the acquiring company were met; organizational structure deadlines were missed; and terminations, which are endemic to most acquisitions, were randomly occurring. When asked what it felt like to work there, an employee said, "We are numb, frozen, and afraid to do anything." Another employee shared how colleagues were receiving random phone calls informing them of their termination. He likened it to being a victim of a sniper attack: "We don't know when the shots are coming or who will be picked off next." It is easy to see how growth is limited in this type of environment. Chaos is having zero predictability or control over inputs and outcomes. And although more common than Stagnation, it is not an environment to desire, frequent, or reside in.

Order

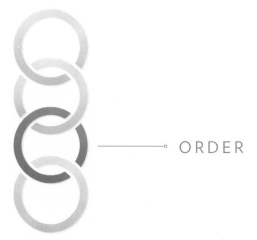

ORDER

Next to Stagnation is *Order*. Order is where people tend to want to exist because it is the most comfortable environment, but it is also the most dangerous. Order is achieved when the same repeated processes lead to a predictable result. However, predictability can lead to comfort and comfort is what can make Order catastrophic.

Doing the same thing with predictable outcomes is attractive in many settings. For example, the process followed by Southwest Airline pilots with an outcome of delivering us to our destination safely creates healthy Order. (However, if new, safer ways to fly a plane were discovered and not adopted, Southwest's Order could quickly turn into Stagnation.) As frequent business travelers, we have developed a detailed process that makes the ordered outcome of our 150-plus trips a year through airports very predictable and tolerable. For every trip, we keep our passport and wallet in the same briefcase sleeve; put our tablet and laptop in their own compartment; place our money clip, purse, glasses, and belt in the X-ray bin; and so on—everything is repeated in the same manner when we navigate airports and airplanes.

Why the repetition? In these examples, the same, consistent inputs lead to predictable, desirable, and repeatable outcomes—Order. Keep in mind the objectives of putting these specific processes in place have nothing to do with growth or advancement. For Southwest, the desired outcome is passenger safety, and that needs to be highly repeatable. So, if the passenger-safety goal is met, the same process is followed. For us, our disciplined travel process ensures that passport, phone, glasses, purse, tablet, and other critical items arrive at our destination with us—the desired outcome—as opposed to leaving them on airplanes or at security checkpoints.

Some years ago, my (Bill's) wife informed me of a new opportunity to make my trips through airport security more efficient. It was called TSA PreCheck. To obtain this qualification would require me to take a trip to the local TSA office (sixty miles away), fill out paperwork, go

continued

through an approval process, and pay a small fee. My response to her suggestion? No! I explained to her how my current process was effective, and I didn't see a need to change it. What I was saying without using the words was that I was entrenched in my Order and comfortable with the outcome.

Fast-forward to a time shortly thereafter when I was late for a flight taking me to a meeting. The security line was long, which created immense stress for me. I wondered if I would miss my plane and the important meeting that awaited. While moving at the typical snail's pace, I watched a smaller line moving more quickly through security. I asked a TSA employee why the other line was so much shorter and moving more quickly, and she responded, "Oh, that line? That is for our TSA PreCheck passengers."

What *was* my best Order now proved to be an inefficient way to navigate airport security. The existing comfort that resulted from predictable outcomes shrouded my opportunity for an improved result. It took an emotional event (the fear of missing my meeting) to bring attention to my antiquated Order, which motivated me to jump through the TSA PreCheck approval hoops, which I did the following week.

Predictable, ordered environments are so desirable, they affect almost everyone's behaviors and daily business practices. Revenue predictability influences share price in publicly traded companies as well as goal setting and budgeting processes. To create more Order throughout our professional careers, we've been required to, and have required others to, create plans—sales plans, professional-development plans, territory plans, and operational plans. The publisher of this book required us to develop an outline, a plan for how the book would be laid out and written. And this is all done with the goal of having repeatable, desirable outcomes. And when predictability is achieved, comfort follows.

However, Order also presents its fair share of challenges. Order, by nature, doesn't promote evolution, and for quite some time science has shown that absence of evolution leads to extinction. Examples of evolution and lack thereof are abundant in the history of our planet. Pesticides that are used to kill insects and plants have been found to be ineffective after several generations (which is a brief period in the insect and plant world). The insects and plants evolve and develop immunities to the poison so they can continue to exist and perpetuate. Another example is the peppered moth, which at one time had a light coloring, but darkened in response to pollution from the industrial revolution. This mutation came about because the light-colored moths were seen and eaten by birds more readily, so with natural selection the dark-colored moths survived to reproduce.

If conditions change faster than a species can evolve, then extinction is the likely result. This applies not only to biology but also to products, markets, skills, and businesses. In your businesses, technology has exacerbated the speed at which Order morphs to Stagnation, and we see nothing that indicates this will slow down. Order that does not evolve is a threat to everything: land and water, our bodies, our governments, and certainly the department or team that you coach. Take the story of Blockbuster Video, a popular and successful business in its time. It's a worldwide example of how sticking to the comfort of Order can ruin your business. Here is an overview of the timeline of events leading up to Blockbuster's demise:

> 1985: David Cook opens first Blockbuster in Dallas, Texas
>
> 1987: Blockbuster sold to investors for $18.5 million
>
> 1992: 800 stores worldwide
>
> 1994: Viacom purchases Blockbuster for $8.4 billion
>
> 1997: Reed Hastings is charged $40 late fee for tardy return of a movie, which motivates him to create Netflix
>
> 1999: Viacom takes Blockbuster public

2000: Blockbuster brings in almost $800 million of revenue
... in late fees

2000: Blockbuster turns down offer to buy Netflix for $50 million

2002: Netflix goes public

2004: Blockbuster has 9,094 locations, 84,300 employees,
and $5.9 billion in revenue

2007: Blockbuster CEO steps down

2010: Blockbuster declares bankruptcy

For years, Blockbuster's processes provided them desired, ordered outcomes, but there were signs of technology shifts. Digital streaming, though relatively new in the early 2000s, seems like an obvious threat in hindsight. At a minimum, it should have been seen as a reason to shift the way Blockbuster distributed its movies. But Blockbuster did not do this. It stayed with a process model built on having physical outlets, charging late fees, and making people leave their homes to rent a movie. This indicates that the company made conscious decisions to stay the course, to accept their ordered environment. This does not mean, however, that Blockbuster didn't attempt other models and directions, but they were either executed poorly or did not have enough resources committed to make them successful. And while Blockbuster was floundering, Netflix, though founded twelve years after Blockbuster, was thriving. It is now an $11 billion company. Blockbuster is one of many examples in a long line of businesses that were gobbled up by Order.

Every day, we visit with executive leaders who have no idea they are cemented in Order or that the key to breaking their minimal growth cycle and getting beyond their limiting Order lies in the activities and behaviors of their frontline managers, not their salespeople. Many of these leaders are from large Fortune 500 companies that are stuck in mid- to upper-single-digit sales growth, or they have no ability to grow organic revenue. They sell, train to sell, roll out new products, manage pipelines, and track every activity a salesperson does or doesn't do (an executive leader told us they put GPSs in the cars of their salespeople, so they even know when they stop at a Starbucks) consistently, year after year. They have unknowingly created an ordered environment that develops and executes plans for single-digit growth and nothing more.

One of the most relatable and understandable examples of Order is physiological. Most everyone who exercises understands what the word *plateau* means, especially weight lifters and runners. A runner who measures progress by lowering their time in a 5K race can run the same course, the same days, over and over again, and improve their time. A weight lifter who measures progress by the maximum amount they can bench-press can bench-press four sets a day, three days a week, and improve their maximum lift. This proves that a person can do something repeatedly and realize gain, but only for a period of time. When working with executives in a workshop setting, I walk them through the exercise example and then ask, "If you never change your exercise process or input, what happens?" Their response if always the same: "You plateau." I then ask, "So, what do you need to do to avoid plateauing and always be growing?" The answer is always the same: "Change your routine!"

The negative consequences of Stagnation and Chaos are obvious, but Order, while needed and present in high-growth teams, can be a dangerous ally if not carefully monitored. Coaches need to pay close attention to their own and their team members' behaviors to make sure the outcomes of any ordered work are producing desired results, while simultaneously looking for new and better processes that lead to improved outcomes. Later in the book we will show how Order is effectively used by coaches to enhance or produce a high-growth team. And don't forget that it is the role of the coach to make sure their team doesn't miss the opportunity to sign up for TSA PreCheck.

Complexity

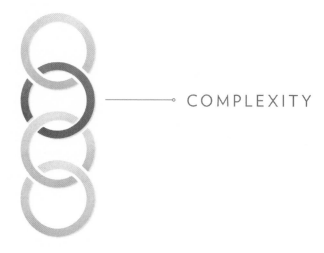

To break the Order, and hence the minimum growth cycle, you need to change what you input. When inputs are altered, you eliminate Order and enter the *Complexity* environment. Understanding this environment, its application, and how it is established or destroyed is critical because *Complexity is the only environment that creates exponential growth or consistently sustains growth.* Everyone, regardless of their life stage or place in their professional journey, needs to comprehend this concept and strive to attain this Growth Ring. And to attain Complexity, you must first understand that it is driven by changed inputs, unknown outcomes, and discomfort.

CHANGED INPUTS

You, your company, or other external factors can cause these changes. In nature, a forest fire would be categorized as a changed input. Physically, a new workout routine is a changed input. Examples in the business world include development of a new product or marketing scheme, a new competitor showing up in your market, local or global economic shifts, application of a coaching methodology, or simply asking a person to do a new task. These are all changed inputs that will lead to altered outcomes.

When I (Bill) worked for Mitch in my first management role, our company had agreed to accept and distribute a new product we'll refer to as *Tech A*, which used a technology that had not been used in mass application. This is an example of a changed input in itself, but Mitch also wanted to change our new product rollout plan by requiring each salesperson to sell ten units of the new product to achieve a bonus. So not only did we have a new product to sell but the salesperson's compensation was also altered in a way that if this new product's minimum sales were not met, the salesperson's income could be drastically reduced. Anytime multiple inputs are changed, outcomes become even less predictable, which then ensures greater downstream disruption.

UNKNOWN OUTCOMES

The impact of entering a complex environment can be immediate, or it can trickle down into the future and create change in ways that are harder to predict. In EcSell's TEDx Talk, "Why Comfort Will Ruin Your Life," we used the story of Claudette Colvin and her unwillingness to give up her seat on a racially segregated bus as a way to illustrate unknown outcomes. She changed an input (not moving from her seat) and perhaps understood she could be in trouble in the short term, but she likely had not thought of the trickle-down effect of her actions—the unknown outcome. Not only did she set the stage for Rosa Parks to do the same, but she couldn't have predicted that she would end up testifying in the famous *Browder v. Gayle* lawsuit before the US Supreme Court. On December 17, 1956, they upheld the United States District Court ruling that the state and local laws requiring bus segregation in Alabama were unconstitutional.

It is important to note that not all Complexity creates desired outcomes. In an article titled "Embracing Complexity" in the September 2011 edition of *Harvard Business Review*, author Tim Sullivan cites an example of park rangers in Yellowstone National Park who brought in the US Cavalry to hand-feed elk in the late 1800s to reduce elk die-off during winter months.[2] Elk were originally a plains animal, but due to westward expansion and modified land-use practices, they were forced into yearlong residence in the mountainous region. However, they had not adapted to the harsh mountain winters, and the population, having already been decimated from an estimated ten million to fifty thousand, was of huge concern. The changed input, hand feeding, was successful and the elk population swelled, but this desired outcome came with an unknown result. Years later the Complexity caused a trickle-down effect of fewer trout. Researchers discovered that elk would feed on aspen trees, which were also used by beavers to create dams. These beaver dams captured the spring runoff, which allowed trout to spawn. The more elk, the fewer aspen trees, the fewer beaver dams, and ultimately the fewer trout. Not a desired outcome, and if you are wondering where the *growth* is, it came in the knowledge scientists gained about the interconnectedness of the elk and their ecosystem.

When most people deliberately trigger Complexity by changing an input, they have a desired outcome in mind. For example, when a new product is introduced to a sales team (creating a changed input), it likely has been developed to meet a specific market need and increase revenue or profitability for a company (the desired outcome).

In our experience with Mitch, the new Tech A product, along with sales minimums and compensation changes, not only caused a great deal of consternation for the entire sales department but also had other, unknown outcomes. What Mitch didn't plan on was how the technology in Tech A would be used in future products for not just our company but also for

---

products distributed by our competitors. Fortunately, because of the challenges we had experienced with Tech A and the resulting intimate knowledge of the technology, our team was more equipped to sell, service, and help our clients maximize all the newest technologies. Thanks to Mitch's willingness to create and stick with the discomfort he caused, we became the dominant player in the distribution of all the new products.

DISCOMFORT

While not all Complexity creates discomfort, all discomfort is caused by Complexity. For example, entering a new market with an existing product may cause extreme discomfort for some salespeople who may immediately think, *Who are our new call points? What will the objections to our product be? Does this market have the same budgets? Do we prospect differently?* And yet other salespeople will respond with little to no discomfort despite not having answers to the same questions. But the same salespeople who are not bothered by the addition of a market may totally lose it if the product being sold is modified. Complexity and the discomfort it creates are unique to us all (which is why it is critical for high-growth coaches to know how Complexity affects everyone on their team).

From physical pain like the sort that comes from a knee replacement to the psychological pain of quitting a bad habit, discomfort is caused by either fear of the unknown or by doing something differently. And because these things create discomfort, they are usually avoided. To think of this in a coaching context, our research shows that 52 percent of managers refuse to accept the discomfort of Complexity (which would require them to coach differently), in spite of the profound evidence that doing so will lead to more sales. Change is hard.

Discomfort provides a wonderful opportunity because of your individual ability to recognize when you feel it. Acknowledging discomfort allows you to analyze its cause, leading you to make a conscious decision to either remain in discomfort, causing Complexity, or go back to Order.

Knowing that exponential and sustained growth only occurs when you are in Complexity forces you to decide to select growth or no growth.

These comfort-versus-discomfort decisions can be conscious or unconscious, and they are not uncommon. Consider your personal health and fitness. Everyone acknowledges that the way they eat and exercise has an effect on the quality and longevity of their lives. When we ask our audiences about lifestyle choices, nine out of ten people indicate they don't eat or exercise properly; probably very few will make the needed changes to live a longer and healthier life. Going to the gym can create psychological discomfort for many reasons: you may feel self-conscious about your body, you may be concerned about how others view your workout routine, or you may feel guilty about not being home with your kids. It also creates physical discomfort when you lift weights or train aerobically—effective weight lifting means that muscle fibers are torn and then become stronger as they heal. Complexity, leading to growth, is at work in your body when you work out.

> KNOWING THAT EXPONENTIAL AND SUSTAINED GROWTH ONLY OCCURS WHEN YOU ARE IN COMPLEXITY FORCES YOU TO DECIDE TO SELECT GROWTH OR NO GROWTH.

With Tech A, Mitch created discomfort right from the start. By changing the new product rollout plan along with salesperson compensation, he made us concerned about many things. We asked ourselves, *Will the new technology work as advertised? Will we have more returns? Will it shake our clients' trust in us? Will the salespeople make less money? Will anybody quit?*

It is safe to say that without the change in the compensation plan, fewer units of the new product would have been sold. What we don't know, however, is whether we would have sold as much of our other products (the salespeople had a portfolio of about ten products to sell) without the addition of the new product. Although there is an obvious correlation, we believe the answer is no. Part of the mystique of Complexity is that there are related outcomes that are hard to track; though these changes happened some years ago, there are still positive and negative trickle-down effects occurring today—and these will continue for many years.

What was once complex can eventually become Order and could even evolve to Stagnation when growth ceases. For instance, our colleague described the first swimming lesson for his son, Alexander, in which the instructor dropped a weighted ring to the bottom of the pool and had the kids go underwater to retrieve the toy. She began by dropping it in very shallow water, then progressively got deeper with each retrieval. At one point she let the ring sink to a depth where Alexander felt uncomfortable, and he turned to her and said, "I can't get that." Alexander had hit the limit of his Complexity. Yet after a few more lessons, not only did he paddle to the bottom to grab the ring, but also, there was not a depth in the pool he was afraid to dive into. What was once complex had become Order, and new ways to challenge Alexander were needed for his growth as a swimmer to continue.

Bill's Personal Growth: Discomfort and Discovery

My youngest daughter spent her senior year of high school at Gomez Tennis Academy, in Naples, Florida (we shared the story of Gomez in the preface). Leaving her home in Lincoln, Nebraska, moving to Naples, and living with a bunch of kids from around the world was a very uncomfortable decision for not just her but also my wife and me. *Our* Order had been for her to finish her schooling up the street where all our other kids graduated. We envisioned celebrating all the usual senior events with her—homecoming, prom, and academic banquets— and we wanted to watch her compete in her final year of high school

continued

tennis. We could have held her back and not let her move to Florida, but that would only have appeased our discomfort, not to mention that keeping her close also would have kept her in Order—limiting her growth in a sport where she so badly wanted to achieve.

For my daughter, moving to Florida and playing tennis eight hours a day was a shock. There was discomfort in her body, but the pain and soreness eventually became Order and ceased. The coaches were very cognizant of pushing players to their limits (into Complexity) and then backing off, bringing Order to the Complexity for days and weeks. When a player began to plateau and their growth slowed, the training was amped up again, creating new discomfort in their bodies and minds. This was repeated at a different pace for each student, but discomfort was created on a regular basis. Complexity is the only way for an athlete to create and sustain growth.

My daughter is now a college junior and has not lived at home since her junior year in high school. Sadly, what was once Complex, having her gone, has become Order for her mom and me.

COACHES MUST EMBRACE AND FACILITATE COMPLEXITY

Complexity's impact, which is to say discomfort's impact, on the performance of individuals and teams is profound. The coach must control this high-growth environment, instigating and perpetuating it when appropriate. Coaches who know their job is to ultimately create and sustain growth will hopefully view discomfort as something to embrace and not avoid. The graph below illustrates how a coach who creates Complexity performs at higher levels. Specifically, in a sales department, coaches who create Complexity have teams that sell more.

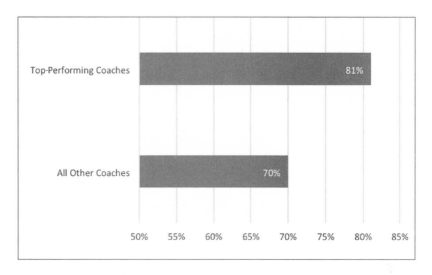

Figure 1. The Mean Complexity Theme score for top-performing coaches (top 20 percent) compared to their coaching peers.

Another common observation in our work is that because discomfort is most often the result of Complexity, very few people want to create or stick with a complex environment. Given what we now know, a great growth lesson has been comprehending the grit it took for Mitch to stick with his tough decisions. He was a master at creating new, challenging disciplines when growth slowed or ceased. There was always an influx of new products, technologies, sales goals, compensation programs, training, certifications, and so on. A person could argue that he caused too much Complexity, which would have been easy to say in the moment. Looking back now, it is clear that he created growth—uncomfortable growth.

It takes a talented frontline or executive leader to know when and how to personalize Complexity for an individual and decide when it is appropriate for a team. More than anything else, a coach must be very strong-willed to have the ability to persevere through discomfort and shoulder all the baggage that comes with the disruption Complexity causes. When those on your team are complaining and when upper management wants to know why there is consternation in your department, even when you question

> EXECUTIVE LEADERS WHO ARE COMMITTED TO EVOLUTION AND WHO DO NOT ACQUIESCE IN CHALLENGING PERIODS CAUSED BY COMPLEXITY SHOW MORE GROWTH.

yourself, do you have the courage to keep going?

According to our research, most managers do not. They find excuses to look for another approach, to return to old ways, to make a popular decision as opposed to doing what is best for the team. For example, we see that coaches in sales who role-play challenging selling scenarios with their salespeople are effective in helping their team members grow. But after a while, many coaches discontinue this exercise, and when they are asked why, they often respond, "My salespeople don't like it." Of course they don't like it; it makes them uncomfortable!

In our work with organizations, we have seen that those that have executive leaders who are committed to evolution and who do not acquiesce in challenging periods caused by Complexity show more growth. We are not saying decisions should never be changed or reversed, especially as new information is uncovered (this is part of evolution as well), but discomfort can cause growth in different ways, many of which will be realized years later.

By now, you are likely wondering if there is a right time to trigger Complexity and how to do it in a healthy manner. Complexity created at the wrong time, the wrong way, and with the wrong people can have a negative impact on discretionary effort, demotivating people to perform. In the coming chapters, we will take a deep dive into a step-by-step coaching process, explore high-growth coaching behavioral themes, and learn how to apply them all in a way that will maximize the performance of your teams. Knowing and implementing this coaching process will provide you the ability to move effectively through the Growth Rings, with an obvious focus on moving into the sweet spot—balancing Order and Complexity.

A final note on Complexity: a person cannot live their entire life in this environment. All of us need Order, and it is healthy to have a balance, with ongoing doses of Complexity and Order. We also wish we could offer a way to know when someone has reached their Complexity threshold or is ready to accept more of it, but for now we accept and are excited about the fact that our coaching discovery journey will likely never end. Although we can provide many fact-based approaches to help you become a great coach, we believe there is still some art to great coaching.

The best news for everyone reading this book is that our research shows that *any* coach who is willing to implement our methods to improve the quantity and quality of their coaching will have teams who grow and perform at higher levels.

#WhatTeamMembersSay

> **Question:** What does your manager do best as a sales coach?
> **Answer:** He truly cares about me as a person. What I have going on in my life and how that fits into work. He knows what I'm working toward in life and encourages me every step of the way.

—Through the Eyes of the Team survey respondent

2

Coaching Redefined

#WhatTeamMembersSay

> "My manager is a great person, but whenever we get to the last week of the month, she makes everyone on the team extremely stressed out. We also have no idea who will show up for the day and what type of mood she will be in, which also causes stress in the team."

—Through the Eyes of the Team survey respondent

THE MOVIE *MONEYBALL* IS based on a book of the same name by Michael Lewis, which tells the true story about how data and strong leadership changed the historic game of baseball. The overriding theme of the plot was how visionary coaching could overcome the financial inequities endemic to professional baseball. An example is the New York Yankees, who in 2002 had an annual budget of approximately $130 million to build and play their team, while the Oakland A's had only $44 million.

At the end of the 2001 season, due to their budget constraints, the Oakland A's lost their top three players to other teams. This exodus, along with the overriding financial injustices inherent to Major League Baseball, caused the Oakland As' general manager, Billy Beane, to search for a new way to acquire, develop, and play talent (hence, coach a team). In the movie, Billy Beane meets a recent college graduate, Peter Brand, who has no prior experience running a baseball team. Despite this obvious shortcoming, Peter, with brutal candor, explains to Billy his thoughts on baseball teams and how they operate in antiquated ways.

Peter says to Billy, "There is an epidemic failure in the game to understand what is truly happening, and it leads people who run major league ball clubs to misjudge their players and mismanage their teams." Peter proposes a new way of analyzing player talent and evaluating team effectiveness, which results in an unorthodox way of fielding a baseball team.

This unique method was the catalyst for Billy Beane's strategy on how to compete with big-money teams, but it was also a departure from the Order baseball had known since the game began. The data that most correlated with scoring runs (hence winning games) were metrics baseball teams were not emphasizing enough when making player-acquisition decisions. Though the data provided the A's with an alternative way to build their team, it also created significant discomfort for the organization as well as the entire league. But the outcome was profound: that year, with a perceived team of lower-tier players, the A's won the most consecutive games in the history of the American Baseball League. Since that time, not only have the Moneyball data concept and resulting method of play been adopted by most Major League Baseball teams, but its core tenets have permeated other sports as well.

DEVELOP YOUR COACHES THE WAY YOU DEVELOP YOUR EMPLOYEES

These days, sales departments could learn a lot from this *Moneyball* example. They are mired in Order. Their performance thinking is medieval and archaic, and there is an "epidemic failure" to understand what creates growth. Why is it that a team can underachieve and then bring in a new coach and achieve significant growth? They altered the input that has the most powerful impact on performance outcomes—the coach. Yet in business, nobody quantifies coaching effectiveness. Executive leaders have forever been viewing incomplete or inaccurate data regarding team performance because they are not looking at the root cause of performance growth—the coach. This is the business version of *Moneyball*.

> EXECUTIVE LEADERS HAVE FOREVER BEEN VIEWING INCOMPLETE OR INACCURATE DATA REGARDING TEAM PERFORMANCE.

Every customer relationship management (CRM) adoption, every technology implementation, all frontline employee and sales training, and anything and everything geared to helping employees become more productive should cease. No more resources should be committed to any frontline workers before the company understands the effectiveness of the coach. Until that happens, the success or failure of any programs, products, or services cannot be accurately measured and understood without knowing if the coach enables or disables performance.

Today, there is little focus and no science-based, measurable approach regarding what a coach should do. When one is promoted to a management role—typically, it is the best individual performer—they are given a team and a goal (hopefully) and told, "Go get 'em, tiger." And while this perhaps sounds ridiculous, this Order plays out across corporations worldwide. We are not insinuating that there are no performance expectations placed on management, and we would argue that the frontline coach is the most challenging position in a company. But the resources for development are given overwhelmingly to the frontline worker or individual performer, rather than the coach leading the team. The outcome of these misplaced resources is increased turnover, low engagement, and lost revenue—revenue executives aren't even aware they are losing, which then masks the proper growth solution.

To further underline the seriousness and naïveté of this narrative, ask yourself the following questions regarding the sales department:

- Do I believe managers need accurate metrics to help salespeople maximize sales growth?

- Do I believe the performance and growth of a team reflects how that team is coached?

If both of the preceding questions were answered in the affirmative, the following table will support the new way team performance data should be viewed.

Again using a sales department as our example, there are four quadrants of data every frontline coach and executive leader should have at their disposal, without which effective decisions regarding how to best grow sales cannot be made. The upper left and lower left quadrants are typically filled with robust data that is customary practice for most sales departments.

Metric Type	Salesperson	
Measure what they do (quantity of their work)	Sales activity	
Measure how well they do it (quality of their work)	Customer feedback Activity ratios Coach's objective feedback	

- Upper left—What salespeople do (the quantity of their work). These are common sales metrics, such as the number of calls made, appointments, presentations made, proposals created, closing calls made, and so on. Most sales departments, large or small, track this critical information because a coach would struggle to coach a salesperson without it.

- Lower left—How well salespeople do their jobs (the quality of their work). Here is where it begins to get tricky. Most coaches simply consider closed deals or progress to a goal a measure of quality. We often hear this from coaches: "If a salesperson hits their number, that tells me everything I need to know about how good they are." While those are accomplishments worthy of reviewing, there are other, more accurate, ways to determine the quality of a salesperson's work, such as surveying customers and having their coaches objectively grade their skills.

Now, let's focus on the right side, blank quadrants . . .

Earlier, we asked two questions. Let's review them:

- Do I believe managers need accurate metrics to help salespeople maximize sales growth?

- Do I believe the performance and growth of a team reflects how that team is coached?

Again, if you answered yes to both, consider this: What is the quantity and quality of the coach's work?

Metric Type	Salesperson	Sales Coach
Measure what they do (quantity of their work)	Sales activity	?
Measure how well they do it (quality of their work)	Customer feedback Activity ratios Coach's objective feedback	?

> EVERY BUSINESS HAS . . . THE OPPORTUNITY TO TRANSFORM AND ELEVATE THE PERFORMANCE OF EVERY EMPLOYEE ON EVERY TEAM.

Our educated guess is that you don't know. Nobody knows. We have shown and explained these data quadrants to more than a thousand business leaders throughout the world, and not a single one of them has said that they track the quantity and quality of their leaders' coaching ability. This further proves the Order in which sales departments are cemented. As a matter of fact, when asked what coaching data they track, most leaders seem perplexed or ashamed and say nothing, but they have a look on their faces that says, "I can't believe I've been missing this my whole career." Knowing and improving the effectiveness of coaching is not just a worldwide growth and performance challenge, but a significant, Complexity-driven, Moneyball type of *opportunity* that every business has—the opportunity to transform and elevate the performance of every employee on every team.

We should also mention that when we fill in the quadrants with coaching data, we see that managers generally do only 44 percent of the activities needed to sustain team growth. We don't believe they are avoiding work; they just don't know what to do or how often to do it. (In the next chapter, we will share what coaching data should fill the upper right and lower right quadrants, which will quantify coaching effectiveness and allow coaches to understand how they are affecting their team's discretionary effort.)

THE COACHING PERFORMANCE EQUATION

More and more, we read articles on LinkedIn and in periodicals such as *Forbes* and *Harvard Business Review* about the need for improved coaching.

There is also a plethora of consultants who tout the virtues and benefits of how coaching affects performance. And this is all positive. These are all ways that people are bringing attention to what we all know— that nothing elevates performance more than coaching.

> NOTHING ELEVATES PERFORMANCE MORE THAN COACHING.

However, in all of our research, we found nothing that defines coaching or promotes research-based (not opinion-based) coaching activities and behaviors that lead to gains in discretionary effort. And there is absolutely nothing that promotes the injection of healthy discomfort or measurement of coaching inputs and outcomes. Justifiably, many pundits are saying, "You need to coach more" or, "You need to coach better," which is similar to telling a sprinter, "You need to run faster." This is simply stating the obvious, and readers are left with no wisdom about how to improve as a coach. Everyone knows that coaches influence performance, but leaders need to know what coaches specifically do that most effectively improves team results.

To begin to answer this challenge, let's turn to the Growth Rings. Because the Growth Rings are our model detailing how environments affect the growth of all living things, it is critical to understand how components of the Growth Rings influence team performance and should be utilized by coaches to create growth for a business team. We are going to assume that every coach or executive leader wants to grow results, because we have never worked with a team that didn't want to improve over the previous year. Nor have we ever worked with or talked to a leader who said, "Our goal is no growth for the coming year."

Though growth is the desired outcome, it is typically stated as a goal— and it is achieved by improving the coaching inputs. To illustrate this, we need to introduce another model—the *Coaching Performance Equation*. This model depicts how the environments of Order and Complexity, along with a new variable, Relationship, affect team performance.

R + O + C = P

(Relationship + Order + Complexity = Performance)

These three business-coaching variables (Relationship, Order, and Complexity) are inextricably linked to your team's performance and are always affected by the way you coach. Knowingly or unknowingly, you have a relationship with each team member who reports to you, the strength of which affects the discretionary effort you receive. Order and Complexity, which exist in many different forms, are created, perpetuated, or minimized by what you do and how well you do it, again resulting in an increase or decrease in team performance.

Details of the activities and behaviors a coach should execute to affect the Order, Complexity, and Relationship variables in the equation will be detailed later, but for now we'll share an overview of each of the three performance variables, beginning with the end in mind.

Performance

The way you coach directly affects your team's output. The output is a measurable result that can and should differ for each business, department, region, or role. In a client-service department, performance may be measured by renewal of accounts; in information technology, performance may be defined as the time it takes to resolve technical issues for clients; for sales teams, performance is typically measured by whether a sales goal is achieved. When we use the term *growth*, we are referring to improvements in team performance.

In chapter 1, we explained why and how the Complexity environment created the most discomfort but also the greatest growth. While that holds true in a business team setting, sustainable, healthy growth occurs when there is a blend of Order and Complexity. Employees on your team cannot spend their entire professional existence in Complexity because too much discomfort can be created and will likely lead to turnover or, eventually, Chaos. Likewise, too much Order limits the growth of a team, or it can lead to Stagnation. So to achieve sustainable team growth, there is a continual need for a coach to create a healthy balance of Complexity *and* Order.

Order

As a coach of a business team, when you think of Order, think of technology, tools, and processes that help you drive more effective and predictable results. A customer relationship management (CRM) or software as a service (SaaS) product that helps you and your team understand client interactions or product penetration are examples of technology and tools that bring healthy Order. Other examples are a sales methodology for acquiring customers, talent-assessment tools for hiring new team members, or marketing calendars for planning product launches. Processes that promote Order may be activities like daily huddles, team meetings, one-to-one meetings, interviewing structures, employee reviews, strategic planning sessions, and so on. Order as a stand-alone environment, however, doesn't result in growth, so Complexity must be present to achieve increases in performance.

> ORDER AS A STAND-ALONE ENVIRONMENT, HOWEVER, DOESN'T RESULT IN GROWTH, SO COMPLEXITY MUST BE PRESENT TO ACHIEVE INCREASES IN PERFORMANCE.

Complexity

Departing from Order and venturing into discomfort is challenging for almost everyone, and it's even harder for coaches to create. But the high-growth coaches (the top 20 percent) are adept at challenging those on their teams in unique ways to foster growth. They are better at holding the members of their team accountable for every aspect of their jobs while modeling the same behavior themselves. High-growth coaches ask for more results, challenge with probing questions, and listen intently; they are objective, candid, and detailed in delivering performance feedback, and they are at their best when under pressure. All of these qualities are indicators of coaches who create and perpetuate environments rich in Complexity for the benefit of their team. But here is the rub: Complexity is not nor will it ever be a healthy and sustainable environment without first creating strong relationships with those on your team.

Relationship

Like Order and Complexity, the strength of the Relationship you have with those on your team directly influences performance. Within the Coaching Performance Equation, we define relationships as *establishing trust connections with those on your team.* The strength of relationships is a measurable component of coaching, like Order and Complexity, and can be developed by any manager willing to change how they work with those on their team.

Trust-based relationships are affected in many ways: Do you always do what you say you will do? Do you take the time to get to know each member on your team? Do you care about each member as a person and not just an employee? Do those on your team feel like you help them progress toward their career goals? While you may answer in the affirmative to all these questions, what matters most is how those on your team would answer them—which proves a need to survey for accurate feedback (more on this in the following chapter).

Relationships provide the foundation that allows coaches to create more Order or Complexity, whichever is needed at a given time, in a healthy manner. We continue to use the word *healthy* because if there is no trust in your coach–team member Relationship, you are likely creating a toxic, unhealthy

IF THERE IS NO TRUST IN YOUR COACH–TEAM
MEMBER RELATIONSHIP, YOU ARE LIKELY
CREATING A TOXIC, UNHEALTHY STAGNATION
OR CHAOS ENVIRONMENT.

Stagnation or Chaos environment. Let's say you need a team member to take on a new task: Do you know the person well enough to understand if their talents are a fit to effectively accomplish that task? Do you know their career goals well enough to tie the task into their career development? Do they trust you in a way that, in spite of the unknown, they believe you have their best interest at heart and will do what you say? Developing a trusting Relationship allows you to know what creates Order and Complexity for each member on your team, because what is Order to one may be Complexity to another. And great coaches know what unique buttons to push or levers to pull for each of their team members.

The Impact of Relationships on Discretionary Effort

Across the EcSell parking lot and up a flight of stairs is a local convenience mart called Super C. Super C sits in a primarily residential neighborhood with no major thoroughfares running past its entrance. It is a typical convenience store with gas pumps in front and a variety of basic grocery needs inside. However, for more than twenty-five years, there was one variable that distinguished the 33rd Street Super C location from every other c-mart in town: Barb, the manager.

Barb was not an executive or owner, but she worked for the company for thirty-one years, twenty-seven of which were at the 33rd

continued

Street location. Barb was a master at developing relationships with her customers, and in return her customers bent over backward to help her run the store. She was candid, loving, urgent, inquisitive, and tough, and those of us who frequented her store adored her.

The physical structure of her store was not too unique; however, it was one of the few that had a small area that accommodated eating and drinking. There were four booths in the corner, which was the neighborhood gathering place. Every morning, somewhere between five and twenty-five people crammed into and around the booths drinking one of the roughly eight flavors of gas station coffee. She kept old card table chairs stacked against the wall for overflow. Those who would frequent the booths were politicians and factory workers, men and women, able-bodied and disabled, gay and straight, working and retired, angry and happy, and more. And all were welcome in Barb's store if they acted like ladies and gentlemen.

Barb arrived at approximately 4:30 a.m. to prep for the 5:30 opening. She prepared all flavors of coffee, put doughnuts on the rack, and readied the store for the early crowd. As the booths were filled and the coffee drained, Barb would not be asked to make more coffee. She had already instructed her customers to brew more coffee when the pots were empty. If someone said, "Barb, you are out of dark roast," she would teach them how to brew more. Those who sat in her store weren't required to pay until they got up to leave, and she expected her customers to keep track of what they ate and drank when it was time to "settle up." She carried multiple newspapers, and anyone who sat could pull one from the stack and read it for free—but only if it was folded neatly and returned to the pile. She would remind us that other customers would purchase them, and they needed to look new.

One wintry morning, when the "on the way to work and school" crowd had come and gone, the snow, slush, and mud that had been tracked into the store was unappealing to the regulars who sat in the booths. So they asked Barb to place a mop and bucket next to the door, so throughout the morning and on every snowy day following, they could mop her floor. The engagement and reciprocal trust she created with her customers also reached the cash register. When a customer needed fuel and removed the handle from one of the pumps out front, the cash register emitted a beeping prompt and then required someone to enter a code on the keypad to clear the system and send gas to the pump. If Barb wasn't behind the counter when this noise began, she would scream, "Somebody get that!" and a customer who had been previously trained would be expected to jump behind the counter and clear the register. (I was "certified" by Barb to assist with this task.)

She had an attitude of "It takes a village to raise a child" and behaved accordingly. She asked children about their schoolwork, grades, and hobbies, and if they didn't say please or thank you, she would remind them. She helped them count money and would often accept less if they came up short for their candy. She would ask her customers for money to buy a coat or food for a child who ventured into her store too many mornings without either. If further evidence is needed, I walked in one afternoon and Barb told me that she needed to talk to me. When I approached the counter, she glanced around the store as if she were going to share some national security secret and, in a whisper, surreptitiously asked about my high school–aged son. "Bill, Will was in here this morning at 10:00. Shouldn't he have been in school?" Needless to say, my son and I had a tough conversation that evening.

Adults who frequented her store were likely stopped and interrogated about where they lived, whether they were they married and had kids, where the kids went to school, what they did for a living, what their spouse did, how often they came into the store, and whether they'd like a cup of coffee (first one on the house) and to sit down with the others.

Barb leveraged the strength of her relationships to get things done to an extent that other store managers could not. The trust she developed allowed her to create more healthy Order (a more effective

continued

process for keeping coffee pots full) as well as healthy Complexity (challenging customers to help her with clearing the cash register). Her trust-based relationships also helped develop extreme amounts of customer loyalty, customer engagement, and discretionary effort.

COACHING EFFECTIVENESS IS MEASURABLE

Now, consider this about Barb's store: How much did she pay her customers to have them help run her store? Zero. The irony is that they paid her for the privilege of engaging in the environment she created.

> COACHES DEVELOP RELATIONSHIPS, ORDER, AND COMPLEXITY TO MAXIMIZE INDIVIDUAL AND TEAM PERFORMANCE.

Those who have a desire to grow want to know what the "Barbs" do that can be replicated. It is virtually impossible to quantify what has not been defined, so the first step is to understand the definition of coaching. As shown earlier, our company has tracked more than one hundred thousand coaching interactions in the workplace, analyzed thousands of executive leaders and managers, and surveyed thousands of salespeople and other employees to get a robust view of what drives performance of individuals and teams. From this research, we have defined a coach as one who develops Relationships, Order, and Complexity to maximize individual and team performance. Recall the Coaching Performance Equation:

Coaching

$$R + O + C = P$$

Relationship + Order + Complexity = Performance

Coaching, for almost every organization, has always been considered a soft skill; what differentiates a soft skill from a hard skill is measurability. The way one dresses, their executive presence, social graces, voice intonation, body language, and so on are soft skills because they are not measured nor correlated to performance. Coaching, however, which was once considered a soft skill, no longer fits that definition since it can now be measured and correlated to decreases or increases in performance. For example, when we measure how often a coach does joint work with salespeople, how often they have a career discussion, how often they provide feedback, how often they are holding one-to-one meetings, and how effective they are at all those activities, we can then correlate them to performance and draw fact-based conclusions on coaching effectiveness. With this data, decisions can be made about which performance-enhancing coaching activities and behaviors need to be improved and which bring little or no value and therefore need to be eliminated.

Without accurate insights about what a coach is doing or not doing to

> COACHING, FOR ALMOST EVERY ORGANIZATION, HAS ALWAYS BEEN CONSIDERED A SOFT SKILL; WHAT DIFFERENTIATES A SOFT SKILL FROM A HARD SKILL IS MEASURABILITY.

influence growth, leaders at all levels have a distorted understanding of what performance buttons to push or levers to pull. To achieve growth, managers inevitably place pressure on employees to do more. And in sales, it is the salesperson who is asked to make more calls, have more appointments, create more proposals, build the pipeline, and close more deals. But as Mitch would always say, "There are no such things as salesperson issues, there are only sales coaching issues."

In the introduction, we explained how the outcome of coaching is to create discretionary effort, which is, to reiterate, the additional output produced by a team because of the coach. Because of what they do and how well they do it, certain coaches obtain vast amounts of discretionary effort from those on their teams, while others obtain very little. Navy SEALs produce extreme amounts of discretionary effort because of their commanders and leaders. The SEALs have a saying in which they passionately believe: "There are no bad teams, only bad leaders."

Jocko Willink, a former SEAL, and I met when we both delivered our TEDx Talks at the University of Nevada. His talk and a book he coauthored with another SEAL, Leif Babin, were both titled *Extreme Ownership*. In their book, the authors shared a story of a SEAL exercise during Basic Underwater Demolition training: SEAL candidates were given a series of exercises that involved maneuvering two-hundred-pound rubber rafts on land and sea. Each team's most senior ranking sailor was accountable for obtaining and disseminating the information from the lead instructor and then getting the team to execute it. During several rounds of executing the exercise, one team consistently finished first and another finished last.

Eventually, the instructor asked the leader of the first-place boat to command the poorest-performing boat and vice versa. As you may have expected, the team that had been bringing up the rear won the race nearly every time with the new leader. The former first-place team became a middle-of-the-road performer with its new leader (basically proving that a high-performing team, for periods of time, can overcome poor coaching).

Most executive leaders aren't so naïve to think that all their frontline coaches are great. As a matter of fact, most tell us that they know they have some poor leaders—but do they know how poor? In the SEALs example, the high-performing leader obtained greater discretionary effort, resulting in consistently better performance. But the low-performing commander withheld or limited the performance of his crew: he created negative discretionary effort. A sales team with a coach who produces negative discretionary effort would likely sell more if it were to operate without that manager. As mentioned in the introduction, in our research we found that 30 percent of coaches provide no or negative discretionary effort, which was surprising. Not long ago, we visited with a vice president of sales who had a series of four regions across the country, each with about eight salespeople who reported to a coach of that region. All the teams were struggling to hit numbers except for one—the team whose coach had been released six months prior and who had been operating without one.

The cost of a bad coach, depending on the company, results in millions of dollars in lost revenue. The sad part is that likely one out of three coaches in every organization is weak—and nobody is identifying who they are. But what is worse is that the poor coaches have no resources or understanding of how to improve. All the while, low engagement, turnover, lost sales, and lost productivity pollute the organization.

> THE COST OF A BAD COACH, DEPENDING ON THE COMPANY, RESULTS IN MILLIONS OF DOLLARS IN LOST REVENUE.

For organizations to grow and sustain that growth, development programming with measurable outcomes needs to shift to the leadership team, with a strong emphasis on frontline coaches. Businesses have forever tracked financial information with amazing accuracy. They have learned to track client buying patterns, market trends, inventory turn, price trends, and so much more, all with the understanding that with accurate information outcomes can be affected. Yet it is ludicrous to think that nobody has *any* measurable data on the role that has the biggest impact on the performance of individuals and teams—the frontline coaches.

What seems to exacerbate the coaching naïveté in sales departments, specifically, is that leaders are continually led astray by technologies and services that focus only on the performance of salespeople. These new shiny objects are always at the forefront of conferences and trade shows and account for much of the budget increases requested by executive leaders. But the reality is, the success of a new technology or service is contingent on the coach's willingness to drive implementation of the technology or service. For example, we have visited with countless sales training consultants who say the success of their training work with salespeople is most influenced by the coach's role in reinforcement. And again, nobody knows what coaches are doing or how well they are doing it.

In our opening *Moneyball* example, new data shed light on how a baseball team could win more games. For us, quantifying coaching effectiveness brought a performance-enhancing view that nobody has seen; with this new information, leaders at all levels can have data that objectively shows how coaches are influencing the performance and growth of their teams.

A QUICK WORD ON DATA: as you can tell by now, we love data. But data, as it applies to human behavior and performance, is only worthy if it is used to make decisions about how a person can grow. Too often we see data accumulated and not used, such as output from CRM software. Done

> DATA, AS IT
> APPLIES TO HUMAN
> BEHAVIOR AND
> PERFORMANCE, IS
> ONLY WORTHY IF
> IT IS USED TO MAKE
> DECISIONS ABOUT
> HOW A PERSON
> CAN GROW.

correctly, coaches in sales departments could extract selling data from their CRM program that provides keen developmental insights. With properly aggregated data, a coach should be able to dissect selling skill and activity needs as well as come to some conclusions about selling quality. The fact this is not done more frequently is baffling, especially considering what we know about performance in athletics. There is not a football program in the land (high school, college, or pro) that doesn't track quarterback statistics and then use those stats to further develop the QB's skills. Sales departments have the same opportunity, but our research shows that not only are they not doing it with enough regularity but they also don't even know if coaching happens!

#WhatTeamMembersSay

"My manager comes to the table with an overwhelmingly positive attitude. He is super motivating and wants the whole team to win together. He brings great ideas to the table and ensures that we are well educated on the latest and greatest solutions."

—Through the Eyes of the Team survey respondent

3

Coaching Quantity and Coaching Quality

#WhatTeamMembersSay

> "I have never received feedback or coaching from my manager. She will make herself available for a customer call. That is probably the only skill she has beyond her former sales rep skills."

—*Through the Eyes of the Team survey respondent*

SHARI IS PROUD TO have earned the executive vice president of sales title after sixteen years with her company. She knows it wasn't tenure that allowed her to ascend but more her willingness to ethically do what it takes to always hit her number. It was mildly amusing to her that so many of her early management colleagues (only a couple of whom still work with her) thought hanging around the home office, making their faces known, was the supposed path to senior leadership roles. Shari's approach was much different: after her first promotion to district manager, she didn't want to hang out at the home office; she felt most at home in the field, working with her *salespeople. She loved sales and wanted to make sure those on her team were as passionate as she was about engaging with customers and prospects. If the executives didn't recognize that, then she would take her talents elsewhere— but it paid off.*

It's now budgeting season, and the sales department has been asked to produce a bigger number next year. The growth mandate was expected and comes every year, so it's no surprise; but today Shari contemplates the never-ending cycle of growing sales. She stares at her computer screen and wonders how much more they can ask of the salespeople, while remembering her time in the field and how it felt to always be expected to sell more. She chuckles to herself, thinking about how she has grown since her early days as a sales rep when she blindly tore into her territory and didn't think about, or even care much about, anything other than selling. And how proud of herself she was after that first promotion and for using the same tenacity in driving her team to success. Her management philosophy those early years was simple: she never asked her team to give more than she was willing to give, and no excuses were accepted. The president and board have since acknowledged these as key strengths that helped her climb the internal ladder.

But now it is different: as an exec, there is much more to consider, and decisions must be weighed differently. In addition to forcing herself to be more patient, Shari needs to remind herself, and her team, to balance the needs of the company, employees, and customers. She again smiles and considers the attitude contrast of the "sales rep Shari" versus the "EVP Shari"— it is amazing how today her world looks so different.

The memories are disrupted when her cell phone rings. Yes, it rings, like the phones in her parents' home. She always thought it silly that so many of the salespeople have "rings" that mimic ducks quacking or that replay some song only her kids would recognize. She looks down and sees it is John, the manager of the southwest region. She'll answer that call.

John has been identified as a "high potential" for senior leadership and is also Shari's favorite manager for many reasons, not the least of which is that his team always achieves its goal. She would like to mirror his attitude, skills, and talent throughout the rest of her management team and often wonders how nice it would be to quantify all he does that separates him from the pack. Seeing his name on her phone again makes her smile, for she knows he is responding to an email she sent to her management team that morning asking for feedback and thoughts about growth opportunities and obstacles for next year. He is always the first to respond, another reason she so respects him. But this time the call is different . . .

"Shari, I've been thinking hard about how to grow this year." This is a bit unusual for him to open so directly; he always asks about one of Shari's kids, where she's traveling next, or something other than business. John is a master at crawling inside people's lives and getting them to trust him. So when he jumps right into business, she adds another item to her mental checklist of the talents she believes make him so good. "I've been looking at the sales metrics for my team, I've reviewed them sideways, upside down, and even standing on my head to figure out how to hit our 11 percent growth nut next year. And what I've realized is that I'm looking at this all wrong! All we ever care about or measure is what the salespeople are doing. Think about it, Shari: we know when our salespeople stop at a Starbucks or get a doughnut, we have every metric imaginable on almost every interaction they have with a client or prospect, but here is my epiphany. Shari, how the salespeople perform, how much they sell, reflects what I do or don't do, and if that's the case, then here is the bottom line." John is also a bottom-line person, another item already on Shari's checklist. "Shari, what do I need to do to get my team to sell more? What do I need to do more of or maybe less of? What are my coaching key performance indicators?"

Shari takes a breath, turns to her computer screen, and thinks about his question. While she could come back with some thoughts and opinions, or even probe further, she likes to be as brutally candid with him as he always is with her, so she pauses for a moment and reluctantly says something she rarely says—

"John, I don't know."

....

EVERY DAY, WE VISIT with sales leaders who "don't know," so they judge manager effectiveness in an elementary way—whether the team goal was achieved. And while goal attainment is perhaps the ultimate metric, it is a lagging indicator of coaching performance. John was coaching in ways others were not. What he was doing or not doing needed to be understood not only to help him achieve higher levels of coaching effectiveness, but so that his behaviors and actions could be mirrored by other coaches.

> WHILE GOAL ATTAINMENT IS PERHAPS THE ULTIMATE METRIC, IT IS A LAGGING INDICATOR OF COACHING PERFORMANCE.

What does high-growth coaching look like in action? How does a coach affect discretionary effort? What gets salespeople to sell more? What could Shari have told John? It invariably boils down to two performance indices from which all team results are derived: the *quantity* of coaching and the *quality* of coaching.

QUANTITY OF COACHING

The quantity at which an activity or input is executed is a measure that has practical application to most everything in life. However, what determines whether an activity is quantified is the *perceived* importance of the activity's outcome.

If the life span of a decorative plant in your office is of little importance or consequence to you, there is a small chance that you track the frequency of watering. But consider your automobile, the life span of which you value highly: you track the oil change frequency closely by a time stamp and mileage indicator stuck to your windshield. The more important the outcome, the greater the need to understand the quantity of inputs.

In high-performance or professional sports, in which the outcome is deemed very important (usually defined as winning), quantity measurements are routine. The frequency at which a football team runs versus throws, the number of putts per green for a golfer, the number of shots on goal in soccer, and the number of shots per game players take in basketball are common examples of quantity measurements. The number of repetitions one does lifting weights, the frequency of workouts, the miles a runner runs, and so on are other examples of activity inputs that are regularly measured. The objective of measuring an activity or input is simple: if you know the frequency of an input and can measure the resulting outcome, you can then affect the outcome in a positive manner.

In business, and specifically in sales, where results are almost always considered critical, mechanisms for tracking a salesperson's quantity of work have been in place for years. These are usually defined as "activity measurements." As shown in chapter 2, the quantity of a salesperson's work is tracked by almost every company. The reason is obvious: sales activity data can be used by the company, coach, and salesperson to help understand and direct attention to actions that drive improved results. Simplistically, if a salesperson sees three clients or prospects per day and achieves 100 percent of their goal but needs to grow their business the following year, one of three primary actions must be taken:

1. Increase the number of calls with clients or prospects

2. Improve the quality of calls with clients or prospects

3. A combination of the two

But as also explained in chapter 2, for coaches there is little understanding and certainly no quantification of their coaching activity or coaching inputs. This lack of performance data is odd, considering that the average coach is accountable for $14 million in revenue production and the average salesperson is accountable for $2 million. Coaching inputs are not tracked for a variety of reasons. Here are three possible reasons:

1. Lack of belief that a coach affects the performance of a team

2. No understanding of what coaching activities lead to the greatest team performance, and thus not knowing what to quantify

3. Nobody ever thought of doing this

Since we've already disproved the first of these, the answer must be a combination of the other two, which is important to understand because this assists executive leaders with comprehending the obstacles they face when they implement a coaching process. (We'll share more about obstacles to coaching success later.)

As we explained when sharing the Coaching Performance Equation, healthy Order is needed in creating a top-performing, high-growth coaching environment. And you likely have implemented a good bit of Order, which is reflected in a variety of processes you follow and tools you currently use. However, when referring to high-growth coaching, there are a series of activities that need to be followed for an outcome of improved team performance.

Our research points to four high-growth coaching activities that have the strongest correlation to discretionary effort. This means that, of all the tasks and duties that a coach can perform in a week, month, or year (and there are

OF ALL THE TASKS AND DUTIES THAT A COACH CAN PERFORM IN A WEEK, MONTH, OR YEAR (AND THERE ARE MANY), THESE FOUR ARE THE MOST IMPORTANT.

many), these four are the most important. Think of them as the base of a pyramid on which greater growth can be built. Their importance is so significant, each will be discussed in separate chapters, but below is a preview.

1. One-to-one meetings—consistent, structured, individual meetings with your team members

2. Team meetings—consistent, structured meetings with everyone on your team

3. Performance feedback—objectively documented analysis of an individual's ability to demonstrate the key skills that are proven necessary to role success

4. Career-development plans—individual sessions with team members to discuss, prepare, and document career growth

Note that when we review the quantity of coaching, we measure it two ways: the first is through surveys with team members that specifically ask them the frequency with which these high-growth activities are performed, and the second is through our coaching cloud software. The software allows coaches to execute the coaching activity in a single platform for all members on their team. For example, after a one-to-one meeting is held, the coach can enter notes from the meeting in the coaching cloud software and mark the coaching activity as completed. Likewise, after a team member completes important work, their coach should provide documented feedback on the skills and abilities of the team member needs to complete their work effectively. This objective feedback is entered into the coaching cloud, which allows us to measure how often these critical coaching activities occur. And as you likely have concluded, when everyone is entering coaching activity into a single source, the performance research data points are endless.

These four high-growth coaching activities, for most, should not be revolutionary and are perhaps perceived as commonsense practices for businesses. But what we have found is that *nobody* with whom we have visited understands the importance of the following criteria in regard to the four high-growth coaching activities.

Frequency of high-growth activities (quantity of coaching)

Are one-to-ones being held weekly, monthly, or quarterly? Is performance feedback occurring monthly, quarterly, or at all? Is feedback documented or just verbal? Are coaches discussing career development with team members consistently? Do some coaches do more of it than others? We see vast differences in the quantity of coaching that occurs within companies as well as across companies. One organization may have a coach who fulfills 100 percent of the coaching activities while another does zero.

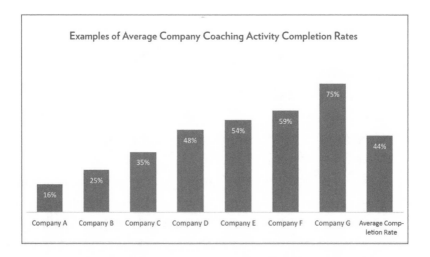

Now consider this: we regularly hear from frontline coaches that they do one-to-ones with everyone on their team, and many executive leaders also claim to hold them. Coaches believe they hold meetings with 90–95

percent regularity; however, when we ask frontline employees how often one-to-ones are held, their perception is that they are *not* held approximately 55 percent of the time. That's a big perception gap. When we study what actually happens, we see that one-to-ones are held approximately 60 percent of the time. Four out of ten times, the ability to create discretionary effort through one-to-ones is wasted by coaches.

In sales, we know that all executive leaders expect frontline coaches to do joint work or ride-alongs with salespeople, yet it is rare to have formal expectations around this activity, let alone see it quantified. For example, we frequently hear from executive leaders that frontline coaches should be spending a minimum of three days per week with their salespeople, but they have no data to support how often this actually occurs. Also, when doing joint work or ride-alongs, are coaches only going on closing calls with salespeople? If the metrics show that the highest-performing coaches are spending 70 percent of their joint work or ride-alongs when client or prospect needs are being uncovered, but you see coaches of teams not at goal are spending 70 percent of their time helping salespeople close client or prospect deals, it is time to change some coaching inputs. Finally, how often do coaches take over a sales call when working with salespeople (the biggest complaint of salespeople)? These are all examples of data points every coach at every level should have at their fingertips.

Who is participating in high-growth activities?

Are coaches spending 80 percent of their time with the lowest-performing 20 percent of their team? Are their top performers getting their fair share of coaching time? (In sales departments, it is common for top sales producers to be left alone because they are hitting their goals—one of the most ridiculous yet common attitudes we see.) Should new team members get more coaching time than the other members of a team? Is it wise for a coach to also have interactions with key clients and accounts?

Again, nobody is tracking these things, which is to say that nobody

> WITHOUT KNOWING HOW MANY OF THE HIGH-GROWTH
> COACHING ACTIVITIES ARE TAKING PLACE OR WITH WHOM,
> NO EXECUTIVE CAN ACCURATELY SELF-DIAGNOSE OR PROVIDE
> FACT-BASED ADVICE ON HOW A COACH CAN IMPROVE.

is quantifying their coaching. Without knowing how many of the high-growth coaching activities are taking place or with whom, no executive can accurately self-diagnose or provide fact-based advice on how a coach can improve.

To provide some scale, the graph that follows shows how frequently high-growth coaches execute high-growth activities as opposed to the bottom 80 percent of coaches.

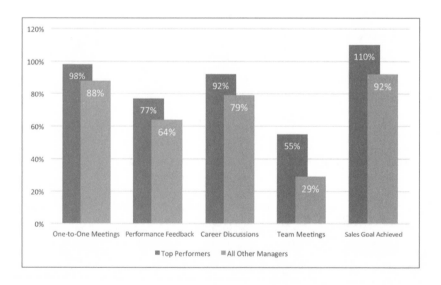

Common sense dictates that when coaches have quantity data like that in the graph, they can self-diagnose and improve team results simply by redirecting their activity. Executive leaders can now measure the quantity of coaching that occurs, which provides them a fact-based way to coach a coach. This is critical, because what we've learned is that while even coaches don't always do what they are trained to do, most will do what they are coached to do.

The desire and need to understand the quantity of coaching that occurs is clear, but what our research shows is more important is *how well* a coach executes the high-growth activities.

QUALITY OF COACHING

Though quantity of coaching and quality of coaching are inextricably linked, we see stronger correlations between *quality* of coaching and how well a team performs than we do with *quantity* of coaching. In other words, coaches who improve the quality of their coaching lead teams who grow their performance levels faster than those who only boost the quantity of their coaching.

But they are linked because we haven't seen a team of coaches improve their quality and grow performance without also increasing the amount of coaching. Likewise, the opposite is also true: we have seen coaches increase quantity of coaching without improving quality—and measurable performance results went backward. What this tells us is that when bad coaches increase their coaching, they are creating more negative discretionary effort.

We recently analyzed the growth of a sales management team within a single company over a twenty-month period. The managers had all received the same coaching training and ongoing developmental resources. We tracked the coaching quantity and quality of this group as well as the sales produced by their respective teams. We separated the results by managers who grew the quality of their coaching over that period versus those who did not (those who had a less than 1 percent increase in coaching quality).

We then looked at how much more coaching was performed by each group as well as the impact on their team's percent to goal.

	Coaching quality	Coaching quantity	Team sales increase
Managers A	+12 percent	+17 percent	+16 percent
Managers B	+1 percent	+12 percent	-9 percent

Managers B, who had a negligible increase in coaching quality but did increase the quantity of their coaching, decreased in their percent to sales goal. Managers A grew both quality and quantity and substantially increased the sales produced by their teams.

The optimal way to measure quality of coaching is to view coaching through the eyes of the team being coached. This is done by surveying and understanding what to look for in the relationship between frontline coaches and frontline workers, or sales coaches and salespeople, or between executive leaders and frontline coaches. We are sometimes asked why we only survey from the bottom up as opposed to the top down or even peer to peer (similar to a 360 review). The answer is simple: nobody is better equipped to communicate coaching insights than those who are being coached. This is analogous to surveying customers if you wish to know the effectiveness of your customer service team. You wouldn't measure the quality of the service your company provides by surveying the customer service team. Logically, you would survey your customers to obtain an objective understanding of *their perception* of your service.

NOBODY IS BETTER EQUIPPED TO COMMUNICATE COACHING INSIGHTS THAN THOSE WHO ARE BEING COACHED.

In order to obtain the best coaching quality feedback, we created a unique survey tool called Through the Eyes of the Team. This is administered by us to employees on a team, so responses can remain anonymous. It is proven that when participants remain unnamed, they provide more honest and accurate responses, which then allow us to poke, prod, and dig to discover what is and is not being done from a coaching perspective. The reported outcomes help coaches, executive leaders, and the EcSell team understand the discretionary effort that is either being positively or negatively created. The results of our findings then provide keen and accurate insights to the coaching dynamic between employees and their bosses. There are two versions of this tool: one is developed for nonmanagerial employees to analyze their boss, and the other is given to managers to provide feedback on the next layer of coaches to whom they report.

From the Through the Eyes of the Team survey, we extract and report valuable data that coaches have never seen nor understood about themselves. It is not uncommon to learn that those on your team may not view you as an excellent coach, or that they don't feel as though you do a good job of recognizing and rewarding their achievements, or that you rarely coach them in a way that stretches their skills, or perhaps that you are just average at motivating them to greater performance. After all the survey information is gathered, we can then create a detailed analysis reported by coach, division, team, and department that not only paints a picture of the existing coaching environment but also shows where improvement is needed. And improvement is always needed.

There are four primary high-growth coaching themes that have been uncovered by surveying and researching more than seven thousand employees across more than two hundred companies—overall coaching, Relationship, Order, and Complexity. Those four primary themes also have eight behavioral sub-themes (two for each primary theme) that make it easier to understand strengths and weaknesses within each. When the anonymous survey is administered, we ask each employee approximately seventy-one questions that allow us to measure behaviors within them for each coach. The survey helps frontline coaches and their executive leaders understand, among many things, the strength of the *Relationship* between coaches and their team members, the levels of accountability a coach creates (Order), and certainly how much discomfort and resulting growth a coach is driving (Complexity).

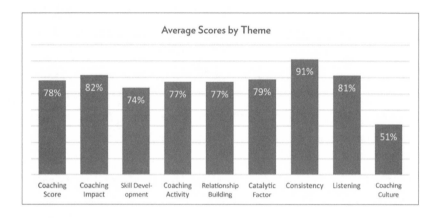

These initial results from the Through the Eyes of the Team survey should serve three purposes:

1. *Create a baseline understanding of how often and how well coaching currently happens.* Through our research, we know that not enough of the right coaching interactions between coaches and their team members occur, and we also know that the interactions that do occur can be improved. An example is that most coaches claim they regularly schedule and hold one-to-one meetings with those on their team. When we ask the team members of those coaches, we get a more accurate understanding of not only whether one-to-ones are held, but the value the team member receives from them.

2. *Analyze coaching strengths and opportunities for growth.* The data that results from the survey provides an in-depth, detailed understanding of what a coach does well and opportunities for growth. Perhaps

a coach scores well in the Relationship theme but, for example, only 34 percent of their team members say their coach has strong follow-through, which would indicate poor Order. Likewise, it is not uncommon to find coaches who score well in the Order theme but low in their ability to drive a healthy discomfort that leads to growth. Every coach we measure can grow their coaching acumen, which is to say every coach has not tapped into the full potential of their team. In sales, 80 percent of the coaches are leaving more than $4 million on the table due to poor coaching.

3. *Personal awareness of one's coaching effectiveness generally creates motivation to improve.* When a coach is given proper feedback detailing information about their coaching effectiveness, it usually creates an emotional event, and emotion drives behavior change significantly more than logic. The feedback should be an eye-opening, humbling, but positive event, resulting in a coach who is now aware of what is needed to grow and improve. Though generally positive, we have experienced the gamut in our feedback sessions—coaches who deny the validity of the survey or their results, coaches who lay the blame on the way questions in the survey are worded, and coaches who say their results are skewed by a person on their team who is unhappy, to name a few. These objections generally come from coaches who have results that are not in line with their own perception of their coaching acumen. The antithesis of this is when coaches accept the results at face value and want to see and hear the good, bad, and ugly. Instead of having a closed mind-set and reacting with denial, they approach the feedback with an open mind-set and desire to learn and grow. While we don't have hard data on how those behaviors during feedback affect coaching improvement, it would seem obvious.

The following is an excerpt from the summary report that explains the different themes and sample questions we ask within each theme.

Through the Eyes of the Team themes

This study summary provides a unique look at management's performance through the eyes of the team members that report to them. The information in this summary, when combined with other relevant performance data, can provide a strong foundation for a frontline manager's professional-development plan.

While other factors are important to successfully leading a team, such as strategic thinking, business decision making, and executive presence, this study focuses on an essential aspect often ignored when assessing management performance—the feedback from team members on how effectively they are coached by their manager.

As mentioned earlier, there are four primary themes—overall coaching, Relationship, Order, and Complexity—and eight sub-themes, the breakdown of which follows.

OVERALL COACHING THEMES:

- Overall coaching impact
- Coaching culture

RELATIONSHIP THEMES:

- Relationship building
- Listening

ORDER THEMES:

- Coaching activity
- Consistency

COMPLEXITY THEMES:

- Skill development
- Catalytic factor

These themes each have questions that go along with them. They were developed by analyzing results of previous versions of EcSell Institute team studies, focus groups with EcSell Institute clients, and third-party research on leadership and coaching. After a thorough review of these sources, EcSell Institute identified these themes as essential to effective coaching of teams. Survey respondents are asked to rate their manager on the questions, typically using a five-point scale, from *strongly agree* to *strongly disagree*.

Following the explanation of each theme, we show examples of the questions that are used. Next to the questions, we put the average score for each response that a coach receives the first time the survey is administered.

PRIMARY THEME: OVERALL COACHING

Sub-theme: Overall coaching impact

Overall coaching impact examines broader, big-picture measures. This theme provides insights on more macro-level components that make a manager a strong coach. It assesses the manager's ability to motivate their team members, use their team members' best skills and abilities, support their team members, and drive enthusiasm for the work being accomplished. It includes team members' comprehensive rating of their manager's overall skills as a coach and leader. Sample questions include the following:

- Your manager is effective at motivating you to greater performance.

- Your manager does a good job of utilizing your best skills and abilities.

Sub-theme: Coaching culture

Like overall coaching impact, coaching culture examines broader, big-picture measures. This theme provides insights into how the overall environment of the workplace is perceived by the team members. Specifically, this theme assesses areas in the team culture that are often outside the immediate control of managers. It also provides an opportunity for senior leadership to understand the elements that affect team performance and that may require their higher level of leadership in order to make changes or improve. Sample questions include the following:

- You would recommend your department to your friends as a great place to work.

- The expectations of your role in this organization are realistic.

PRIMARY THEME: RELATIONSHIP

Sub-theme: Relationship building

Relationship building is a Relationship theme that captures the way managers interact on a personal level with their team members. Included in this theme is a gauge for how comfortably the team members are interacting, sharing, and disagreeing with their manager. It is designed to measure how effective the managers are at creating a partnership of respect, engagement, and rapport. Sample questions include the following:

- Your manager cares about you as a person, not just as an employee.

- Your manager has a good understanding of your personal life goals.

Sub-theme: Listening

Listening is a Relationship theme that provides an indication of managers' ability to listen and connect with their team members. Here, insight is gathered about the verbal and nonverbal signals managers send during their interactions. These indicators center on managers' tendency to either share or dominate personal interactions, as well as the attention they give to their team members when meeting together. Sample questions include the following:

- Your manager does more talking than listening.
- Your manager gives you their full attention when you meet with them.

PRIMARY THEME: ORDER

Sub-theme: Coaching activity

Coaching activity is an Order theme that assesses the consistent and quality execution of essential coaching interactions between managers and their team members. It identifies the frequency of coaching activities like team meetings, one-to-one meetings, feedback conversations, and career discussions. This theme also assesses the quality of these interactions by indicating how beneficial team members find these sessions to increasing their performance. Sample questions include the following:

- How often does your manager hold scheduled one-to-one meetings with you?
- Your scheduled one-to-one meetings with your manager are beneficial.

Sub-theme: Consistency

Consistency is an Order theme that gives a snapshot of a manager's reliability and organizational skills. Within this theme, we gather information about managers' ability to carry out management tasks using consistent, timely, and effective processes. Here, we also gain insights into whether managers are reliable in carrying out their leadership tasks while also setting an expectation for consistent behavior and execution from their team members. Sample questions include the following:

- When your manager says they will do something, they always do it.
- Your manager often asks to reschedule when you have set up a time to meet.

PRIMARY THEME: COMPLEXITY

Sub-theme: Skill development

Skill development is a Complexity theme that captures managers' ability to coach their team members on the fundamental tasks and skills associated with their role. This theme reflects managers' ability to develop their team members' specific skill sets and how they use feedback, educational events, and support to help their team members continue to grow and improve their ability to execute their roles. Sample questions include the following:

- Your manager is more likely to tell you what you did wrong than coach you how to do your job better.
- Your manager is very specific when talking to you about ways to improve your performance.

Sub-theme: Catalytic factor

Catalytic factor is a Complexity theme that measures managers' ability to push team members beyond expected performance. Behaviors associated with this theme include challenging and encouraging team members to work outside their comfort zones while being mindful of not placing excessive stress on them. This theme also measures coaching approaches like providing specific developmental opportunities and giving team members freedom to perform. Sample questions include the following:

- Even when it is sometimes uncomfortable, your manager pushes you to perform at a higher level.
- Your manager purposely asks you to do things that stretch your abilities.

To simplify the measurement and quantification of coaching quality from the seventy-one questions asked, EcSell Institute has developed a single, empirically based number for assessing how well managers perform as coaches. By distilling coaching quality down to a single number, we can measure the relationship between coaching quality and team performance.

There are a series of questions in the Through the Eyes of the Team survey that have been identified as having the strongest statistical relationship to high-growth coaches. Using these questions, a mean percentage is calculated for each manager based on the aggregated feedback from all team members on their team—we call this the manager's Coaching Quality Score. The average score for coaches who take the survey for the first time is 72, a C minus. The average Coaching Quality Score increase after one year of working on coaching improvement is twelve percentage points, taking the average to 84, a solid B. We have seen coaches score as high as 97 and as low as 42.

Indeed, our research shows a statistically significant relationship between managers who demonstrate a higher Coaching Quality Score and teams that more effectively achieve their goals.

COACHING QUANTITY + COACHING QUALITY

When data from coaching quantity and quality are put together and correlated to performance outcomes, we see some remarkable yet expected results. While we expected coaching quality to have a significant impact on overall team performance and growth, we didn't expect small differences in coaching quality to lead to such substantial results. As you can see from the preceding chart, the average difference in coaching quality between high-growth coaches (the top 20 percent) and the bottom 80 percent is only 8 percentage points. We consistently see these small differences across the organizations we research, which tells us that without measuring coaching quality it is hard for anyone to discern poor, good, or great coaching.

Every leader in every company now has the ability to track coaching effectiveness. There is no reason for one out of three managers in a company of any size to be bad at creating discretionary effort. There is no rationalization for employing managers who inhibit team members from performing at top levels. There is no excuse to have leaders at any level who aren't perpetuating growth! Unless organizations and executive leaders want to stick their heads in the sand and ignore the data and research, quantification of coaching performance is available for everyone. Which means becoming a *high-growth coaching* team versus a *manage tasks and metrics* team is now a conscious choice. And if a frontline manager asks, "How do I get my team to perform at higher levels?" nobody will have to respond with, "I don't know."

In the following four chapters, we will be sharing information and research on the high-growth activities. The templates that correspond to these activities can be downloaded from www.ecsellinstitute.com/templates.

#WhatTeamMembersSay

> "She is real. She coaches based on real-life things and not the theoretical sales motions. You can lean on her for coaching and joint sales calls. She will even let you vent when you need to let off some steam. She leads through action, not words, and that makes her team fight tooth and nail for her and the team to succeed."

—*Through the Eyes of the Team survey respondent*

4

One-to-One Meetings

> "Sometimes I feel that during our one-to-one calls she is doing emails and not really listening. She doesn't actually talk to me on a personal level. She hasn't ever asked about me or my family."

—*Through the Eyes of the Team respondent*

Proactive, consistent one-to-one meetings are necessary to generate trust, communication, and accountability with team members. When coaches take the time to connect with team members individually, they get to know their team members better, and they are able to have strategic conversations about how to do their job more effectively. Coaches can help their team members with any questions they may have, assess their progress toward goals, and help them make sure their plans are carried out successfully, holding team members accountable for executing their visions. A regular, effective one-to-one meeting is one of the most important tools a coach has in driving team productivity.

YOU NEED ONE-TO-ONE MEETINGS— EVEN IF YOU THINK YOU DON'T

Many coaches resist one-to-one meetings because they feel they already communicate with their team enough. It's true—most coaches are in regular contact with their team. They may have quick calls to discuss upset customers, or they may reply to an email about pricing concerns. Most coaches have an open-door policy, so people can drop in and talk about issues whenever they feel the need.

> TEAM MEMBERS WHO DON'T OFTEN REACH OUT TO THEIR COACHES WITH QUESTIONS ARE NOT RECEIVING THE INDIVIDUAL TIME THEY NEED.

But here's the rub: according to the coaches themselves, the vast majority of these individual conversations are reactive; they only occur when team members reach out. So the team members who get the most help are the ones who ask for it. This means that the team members who don't often reach out to their coaches with questions are not receiving the individual time they need.

It's the age-old adage at play: the squeaky wheel gets the grease. And the team member who asks for help gets the coaching. Perhaps even more important is that under this reactive approach, nobody is getting strategic time with their coach. Conversations are usually isolated to specific, narrow issues. The team member has a certain question or concern with which they want their coach's help, so the conversation just addresses that limited issue. There's rarely a discussion about team members' overall goals, priorities, and development needs. There is certainly no concerted effort in these conversations to drive career development or push a team member into the Complexity zone, which creates growth in the individual. This leads to most individual coaching being highly tactical rather than strategic. This is also where a regular, proactive one-to-one meeting can make a difference.

A Coaching Success Story

A few years ago, we were working with a management team at a small manufacturing company. They had a supportive but relaxed coaching culture. Team members had lots of experience and therefore reached out to their coaches only when they needed their help on a specific issue, and coaches were responsive when someone needed help. There was little formal coaching, as leaders only held structured, scheduled one-to-one meetings quarterly. In those meetings, they focused mainly on updating metrics and sales targets. At the start of our working relationship with this company, our surveys showed that team members thought their coaches were supportive but also that they weren't getting much strategic guidance.

We began by partnering with them and setting an expectation of how often these one-to-one meetings would happen. (For them, the right frequency was monthly.) Then, we agreed on an agenda for the topics they would cover in the meetings. Next, we shared our research on the coaching behaviors that made one-to-one meetings most effective. Finally, the coaches used our coaching software to execute and track their interactions with their team members.

Soon after changing their approach to their one-to-one meetings, the coaches reported a marked difference in their interactions with their team members. They felt like they were communicating more openly and having more substantive conversations. Perhaps more importantly, their team members felt like they were receiving better coaching. As one of the coaches told us, "My team member said to me this was the best one-to-one meeting we've ever had."

After a year, we surveyed their team members again to get their perspective on how coaching felt different to them. Before instituting scheduled, consistent one-to-one meetings, only 28 percent of the team members said they had a one-to-one meeting with their coach at least monthly. Just a year later, that number was all the way up to

continued

68 percent. Coaching quality numbers also rose, particularly in helping team members strategically improve: 13 percent more team members rated their coach as "very strong" at coaching their skills, 14 percent more rated their coach as "very strong" at helping them strategically plan their work, and 21 percent more rated their coach as "very strong" at helping them achieve their career objectives.

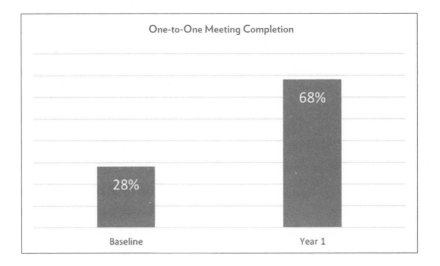

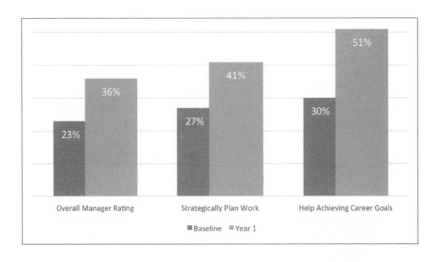

As this company's experience illustrates, regular, structured one-to-one meetings can significantly increase a coach's effectiveness. While coaches usually agree with this idea in theory, they fall short of it in reality. If you are like most coaches, you have dozens of people vying for your time each day. You have a boss that needs an updated report from you. Customers are calling to talk about a product issue. Team members need your help on an upcoming presentation. These are all important, urgent concerns that require your immediate attention. So in the midst of all this, something has got to give. Some of the easiest things to postpone or cancel are your scheduled one-to-one meetings with your team members. But you shouldn't.

Even if you've already talked to your team numerous times or could reschedule because you'd be meeting with them soon, reconsider canceling or postponing. Your scheduled one-to-one meetings with your team members are more important to them and their effectiveness than either of you may have ever realized.

ONE-TO-ONES DIRECTLY AFFECT YOUR TEAMS' PERFORMANCE

According to our Through the Eyes of the Team survey, there is a strong relationship between effective one-to-one meetings and team performance. Specifically, team members who are 11 percent more consistent in having one-to-one meetings with their coaches and rate these meetings 12 percent higher in quality also demonstrate 36 percent more effectiveness in achieving their goals.

TEAM MEMBERS WHO ARE 11 PERCENT MORE CONSISTENT IN HAVING ONE-TO-ONE MEETINGS WITH THEIR COACHES AND RATE THESE MEETINGS 12 PERCENT HIGHER IN QUALITY ALSO DEMONSTRATE 36 PERCENT MORE EFFECTIVENESS IN ACHIEVING THEIR GOALS.

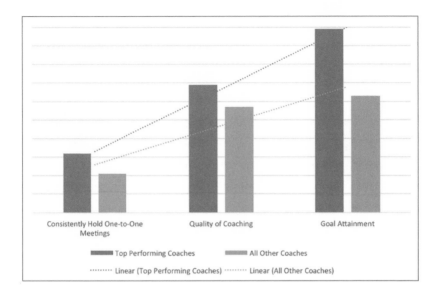

There is a measurable relationship between (a) holding one-to-one meetings consistently and doing them well, and (b) the performance of your team. If you're a coach with a lot on your plate and a calendar full of meetings, don't you want to spend time on the activities that have a measurable impact on performance? One-to-one meetings directly affect performance; they shouldn't be missed.

In this same survey, we found that only 39 percent of team members meet individually with their coaches at least every other week. That means that over half of coaches are not getting the most they could out of their interactions with their team members. And if you're a company or division leader, that means 61 percent of the coaches on your team are missing out on the 36 percent increase in the performance they could inspire in their team members by simply holding consistent, effective one-to-one meetings. Don't leave a huge amount of performance on the table; commit to this coaching best practice.

MAKING ONE-TO-ONE MEETINGS WORK FOR YOU

If you don't want to miss out on the performance improvement your team could achieve, you can begin by committing to consistent, effective one-to-one meetings. But you may have a lot of questions about how to make these meetings most effective. What is the right frequency? What should the agenda for an effective meeting look like? How do you use one-to-one meetings to push your team members into the high-performance zone while also strengthening the trust between you? From our research, we've established some best practices that may help you answer these questions.

Determining frequency

Figuring out the right frequency for one-to-one meetings is a little bit science and a little bit art. When we first began researching recommended frequency of one-to-one meetings, we assumed more meetings would be better and that top coaches would do their one-to-one meetings weekly. One of our biggest surprises was that more meetings don't necessarily yield better results.

In our surveys, we asked team members about how often their coaches conducted scheduled, structured one-to-one meetings with them. Then, we analyzed those responses in comparison to those about their coaches' performance on metrics like goal attainment. When we compared the responses of team members whose coaches were more effective in attaining their goals to those whose coaches were less effective, we were surprised to learn that the one-to-one meeting frequency used by the best-performing coaches was actually every two or more weeks. This trend continued as we studied more coaches and more organizations, and eventually we began to recommend holding these meetings every other week as the preferred standard for our clients.

> MORE MEETINGS DON'T NECESSARILY YIELD BETTER RESULTS.

Now, this is where the art of setting one-to-one meeting frequency comes into play. Many coaches still prefer weekly one-to-ones, feeling it is necessary to their regular communication with their team members. If you feel that way, ask yourself if this frequency is really helpful to your team members or if you're simply doing it out of habit. On the opposite end of the spectrum, some coaches think that doing one-to-one meetings every other week with each of their team members is too much of a time commitment. Again, if this is your feeling, ask yourself if this is really true or if you are simply reluctant to challenge yourself to prioritize individual time with team members over other tasks.

Ultimately, consider what's best for your team members and what is most likely to help them. While a newer team member may want to touch base frequently, some of your most seasoned team members may not need such regular dialogue. Some of your team members may simply want more communication than others. You have to know your team to determine the best meeting frequency for you, but always bear in mind what the research says.

Following through

Of course, it's important for coaches not only to figure out the right frequency for one-to-one meetings but also to actually follow through. Keeping their commitments to their one-to-one meeting schedule is often a coach's biggest challenge. Unexpected issues pop up every day, and everything from an upset customer to an urgent boss to a stressed colleague can cause a coach to cancel or reschedule one-to-ones. Unfortunately, every time a coach does this, they send a signal to their team members that their

TEAM MEMBERS NOTICE WHEN A COACH CANCELS THEIR ONE-TO-ONE MEETINGS, AND THEY JUDGE THE IMPORTANCE OF THESE MEETINGS AND THEIR VALUE AS A MEMBER OF THE TEAM ACCORDINGLY.

one-to-one meetings are not as important as other issues that often arise. Team members notice when a coach cancels their one-to-one meetings, and they judge the importance of these meetings and their value as a member of the team accordingly.

As a coach, if you want to emphasize the importance of your one-to-one meetings and your team members, you have to execute them as consistently as possible. We have found that the easiest way to ensure consistency is to put your one-to-one meetings on your calendar as a recurring event. If a meeting is already on your calendar, you're less likely to miss it. And if you need to move it, you're more likely to reschedule a meeting that was already on your calendar. Plus, a regular cadence for your one-to-one meetings allows you and your team members to plan other work around them. Most importantly, a regular cadence ensures that you do not let several weeks go by without taking advantage of an activity that drives the productivity of the people you lead. The following are important guidelines to keep in mind when it comes to one-to-one meetings.

SET AN AGENDA

Once you have determined the ideal frequency for your one-to-one meetings and have committed to following through with them, the next step is to figure out what you should cover with your team members during the meetings. Most coaches have participated in enough one-to-one meetings to know that the wrong agenda can make a meeting feel boring, repetitive, and even useless. However, the right agenda can help increase communication, camaraderie, engagement, and productivity.

Unfortunately, most coaches make the mistake of using their one-to-one meetings simply to touch base on their team members' current priorities and tasks. The meeting agenda, if they have one, is filled with updates on customers, projects, and internal priorities. But rarely does it address the team member's work on a more holistic level—their bigger-picture concerns, their developmental needs, or their personal goals. This leaves the one-to-one meeting being merely a tactical update of current work rather than a strategic discussion of ways for the team member to develop and improve their performance.

To get the most value from your one-to-one meetings, you need to first fine-tune what you discuss during them. Shift the focus away from only talking about current projects and priorities. Don't just ask for status updates on your team members' work. Stop the dialogue from being merely tactical. You can do this by using a consistent agenda that is more developmental and strategic and has the needs of your team members at the center. A few best practices that we recommend in regard to the agenda of your one-to-ones are focusing on personal updates, checking in on long-term goals, asking your team members about their daily work and activities, and asking your team members how you can help them.

FOCUS ON PERSONAL UPDATES

Always begin your one-to-one meetings by asking your team members about what's going on with them personally. This can be a simple check-in such as, "Hey, how was your weekend?" Or touch base on what they care about by asking, "How was your daughter's soccer game?" Or try to connect with them about their hobbies or personal goals by asking, "How is your landscaping project coming along?"

You may read these questions and wonder if this type of exchange really matters. You may brush them off as simply inconsequential small talk. You may ask yourself, *Do I really need to know this kind of stuff about my team members?* Our research shows unequivocally that you do. In our Through the Eyes of the Team survey, we ask team members to rate whether they feel their coach really cares about them and understands them as a person, not just as an employee. We see that top-performing coaches who are better at attaining their goals are 32 percent more likely to receive the strongest positive marks from their team members on these questions. A way to show that you care about your team members is to know what is going on in their personal lives. It may feel like small talk at times, but getting to know who your team members are outside of work actually has an impact on business outcomes.

Letting your team members know you care about them on a personal level is essential to establishing trust, which will in turn help them grow. How can you possibly encourage your team members to take on challenges outside their comfort zone if they feel you don't even know and care about them as people? Simply stated, you can't.

For some coaches, learning about their team members on a personal level may feel uncomfortable. Maybe they've received advice during their career to not ask personal questions. Maybe they feel like there's too much on their plate to waste time on asking these kinds of questions. Maybe they are simply personally uncomfortable with this level of relationship. But these attitudes will hold them back.

Getting Personal

A few years ago, we were working with a successful consumer foods company. It had outperformed its competition and established its brand effectively in the market, but it wanted to grow at more than its current rate. Their director of sales was trying to figure out how to get his team to engage and perform at a higher level, as they seemed more worried about making mistakes than really pushing themselves. When we gave them our Through the Eyes of the Team survey, we saw a clear reason for this lack of engagement around growth goals. Team members didn't feel like their coach knew or understood them as people.

When we shared these results with the coach, his discomfort in creating personal connections was clear. He asked, "Do you really expect me to get to know my people on this level? Do you know how much time that would take?" Believe it or not, his response was not

continued

uncommon and, in fact, is quite similar to what we've heard many coaches say over the years. Some coaches are simply uncomfortable with what it takes to build genuine relationships of trust with the people they are leading.

It takes time to really get to know your team. And it may not be your natural style as a coach. Personal discomfort with closer relationships may cause you to miss out on this essential element of establishing trust. But even the most reticent coaches can do this if they simply make it part of their one-to-one meeting agenda. Get in the habit of taking five or ten minutes at the beginning of these meetings to spend time connecting on a personal level. It will pay dividends in increasing the connection and trust with your team, which ultimately will drive their engagement.

IF YOU WANT TO ENSURE THAT YOUR TEAM MEMBERS ARE TAKING ACTION ON LONG-TERM GOALS, YOU ABSOLUTELY MUST ASK ABOUT THEM REGULARLY.

CHECK IN ON LONG-TERM GOALS

The next item on your one-to-one agenda should be to ask your team members about the progress they are making toward their strategic goals. Before you get into tactical priorities, you want to first take stock of your team members' progress on a bigger-picture level, as long-term priorities often fall off the radar. Many coaches ask their team members to identify their strategic goals every year but then rarely follow up on their progress. If you want to ensure that your team members are taking action on long-term goals, you absolutely must ask about them regularly. Get their updates on project plans. Look at any performance or progress data you have. Examine where they are doing well and where they are falling behind. This is your chance to coach, counsel, and advise them as they are in the process of completing work that they have identified as strategically important.

Also, don't forget your team members' own development when discussing strategic goals. (Later, we will discuss the importance of holding an annual career discussion and creating a development plan to ensure your team members' continued growth. Specifically, we will focus on how career development drives not only an individual's future growth but also their immediate higher performance.) One-to-one meetings provide a good opportunity to regularly follow up on the development strategies identified in their plan. Follow-up is particularly important with career development, as it can often feel optional in the face of so many other priorities. If a team member misses key performance targets in their work, they will likely face repercussions, but not developing their career is unlikely to lead to consequences. As career development naturally takes the back seat, coaches must work harder to drive it.

Whether driving execution of long-term projects or focusing on a team member's development, one-to-one meetings provide an opportunity for coaches to continually trigger catalytic growth in their team members. Ask your team members not just to focus on the immediate, pressing work in front of them, but to think long term about their growth. Challenge them to take on goals that push them into Complexity. Help them develop by delegating work that requires them to learn a new skill. Most importantly, use your one-to-one time with them to ensure they follow through on these goals.

ASK YOUR TEAM MEMBERS ABOUT
THEIR DAILY WORK AND PRIORITIES

It is undoubtedly important to ask your team members about their daily work. Unfortunately, many coaches spend nearly the entire one-to-one meeting focused on these kinds of topics. While concentrating solely on these day-to-day priorities is too one-dimensional for the entire one-to-one, it is important to address them because they often involve critical customer issues and other time-sensitive matters. You can make these discussions more meaningful by using them to coach your team members' execution and behavior, rather than just ensuring that the work is completed.

The next time you discuss daily work and priorities with a team member, don't just grill them for status updates on projects, customers, or internal matters; ask questions that help them improve their execution. Ask them about how they are approaching a particular project, communicating with colleagues, or ensuring follow-up. Seek to understand the processes they are following and ask them to consider how these processes can be improved. You don't want to be a clipboard manager who just checks items off the to-do list to ensure the work is complete. Instead, you want to be a coach who helps your team members think about and execute their work more effectively. Asking your team members questions about their work processes is the best way to do this.

ASK YOUR TEAM MEMBERS HOW YOU CAN HELP

This last item on your one-to-one meeting agenda is basically an open-ended discussion. Questions, concerns, or frustrations on the part of your team members can keep them from being focused on the more important aspects of their work. Some of our clients refer to this as *mind chatter*, or the worries and issues that keep their minds from focusing. The only way to ease the mind chatter of your team members is to address it regularly. This part of the one-to-one meeting gives them a constant platform to express such thoughts or concerns if they're having them.

It also presents your team members with the opportunity to ask for your help and support. While it may seem obvious that your team members will request your help if they need it, you may coach some individuals who are reluctant to put anything on your plate unless you expressly give them permission to do so. So be sure to let them know it's okay to ask for your help. Creating an open forum in this way encourages them to feel comfortable discussing their needs and issues with you, and it works to strengthen the trust and partnership between the two of you.

Following up

At the end of your one-to-one meetings, it is important to define any necessary follow-up items to ensure that key priorities are addressed before the next meeting. The mistake most coaches make is deciding which issues need a follow-up. This is problematic because it sends the signal that the coach, rather than the team member, is responsible for the follow-up. Defining what actions your team member needs to take before your next meeting automatically puts the ownership on you to make sure these things happen. So one simple change you can make is to ask your team members to define follow-up items themselves at the end of one-to-one meetings.

You may elect to ask your team members for only a verbal recap of follow-up. Or you may prefer for your team members to send you next steps in writing so it's easier to refer to them later. Regardless of the method you choose, it is important that your team members define their own follow-up items so they are the ones who own them. Asking for follow-up is also a good way to make sure you are on the same page regarding what needs to happen. If they give a recap that is different than what you are expecting, it will be immediately clear that you need to clarify. Also, be sure to refer to follow-up notes before your next one-to-one meeting. Defining follow-up is only effective if you actually follow up on it.

EMBRACE THE ONE-TO-ONE MEETING

A one-to-one meeting may seem like a simple thing, but done well it can have a significant impact on your ability to maximize your team's performance.

Conduct these meetings to create regular and effective communication, to strengthen your trust relationship, to ensure tasks are being done consistently, to keep strategic goals on target, to coach how work is executed, and, most importantly, to challenge your team members to develop and grow. If you're already doing one-to-one meetings, use these tweaks to increase their effectiveness. And if you're not doing regular one-to-one meetings, start—so you don't miss out on this important way to improve the performance of your team.

*A one-to-one meeting template can be found at www.ecsellinstitute.com/templates

#WhatTeamMembersSay

> "I really look forward to our one-to-one meetings. I value my time with my manager so much, and having coaching sessions with her helps me stay on track and motivated."

—*Through the Eyes of the Team respondent*

5

Team Meetings

#WhatTeamMembersSay

> "It shouldn't take ten people and three team meetings to screw in a lightbulb."

—Through the Eyes of the Team survey respondent

TEAM MEETINGS—THIS PHRASE CAN create a visceral response in your team members, and it's often not positive. They think of long conference calls in which their manager talks 95 percent of the time. They think of boring updates about performance metrics, or financial results that they already read in their emails. They think of detailed communications about changes to corporate policies or processes. Team meetings are often used as a communication vehicle for leadership within a company, but they are rarely used in ways that could most benefit team members— to help them learn how to do their jobs more effectively.

THE TEAM MEETING DICHOTOMY: NECESSARY BUT BORING

Team meetings present an interesting dichotomy for most coaches. According to our research, nearly all coaches hold team meetings regularly, but few coaches are enthusiastic about them. When we ask coaches how they feel about their team meetings, the phrase *necessary but boring* is what we hear most often.

Coaches know they need to get their team members together on a regular basis to communicate important information, but they are underwhelmed by the engagement they see in their meetings—and team members tend to agree that team meetings could be more effective.

According to our Through the Eyes of the Team surveys, only 29 percent of team members strongly agree that the information they get in team meetings provides great value.

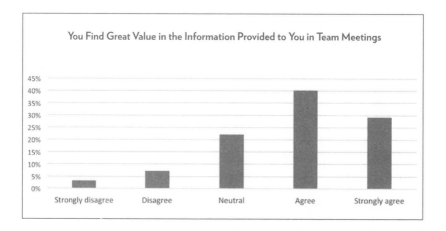

If team meetings are so uninspiring, why do 87 percent of team members report that their coaches hold them at least once a month?

As much as team meetings may not be enthusiastically received, coaches seem to prioritize completing them consistently. So why do coaches hold team meetings? We ask this question regularly in our coaching seminars and hear a variety of reasons. Coaches say team meetings are a way to disseminate information to everyone quickly. Or they use team meetings to ensure everybody hears the same message. Or they say these meetings provide a platform from which to update their teams on key strategies. What's consistent in the coaches' answers is that most of them view a team meeting as a one-way communication vehicle. They want to get a consistent message out, and their team meetings are the preferred way to do so. This isn't a bad reason, but there is so much more that could be achieved on your company's valuable time with a better team meeting.

WHAT DO TEAM MEMBERS NEED FROM A TEAM MEETING?

In our Through the Eyes of the Team surveys, we ask open-ended questions that allow team members to share how their coaches can improve their coaching and management skills. Not surprisingly, improvement of team meetings is a frequent feedback topic.

Here are just a few of the suggestions that team members have shared with us about how their coaches can create better team meetings:

- "Bring in more speakers to monthly meetings."

- "We need more exposure to success stories and idea sharing within the team."

- "Share more best practices."

- "We need more collaboration among my peers."

- "We need better training and more time for training."

The survey comments paint a consistent picture of what team members want from team meetings—more education, more learning, and more training. Whether it's bringing in speakers or sharing best practices among peers, team members see team meetings as a good vehicle to learn strategies they can use to improve and develop their skills. Simply put, team members want information, ideas, and training so they can do their jobs better.

So how can coaches create a team meeting that meets their team members' needs and expectations? How can they change their agenda so the meeting is more than just a communication vehicle? How can they inject more learning opportunities and idea sharing into their team meeting? Making a significant change to the desired outcome, agenda, and structure of their team meetings can provide the necessary improvement.

A Coaching Success Story

Two years ago, we began working with a professional services company that had a large, seasoned workforce. Because it was a publicly traded organization, its leaders were extensively tracking performance metrics and had instituted clear management processes throughout the organization. One of these process expectations was that their coaches complete team meetings on a weekly or every-other-week basis to provide updates on metrics and communicate important company developments.

Although the company didn't have a formal tracking system in place to ensure team meetings were done consistently, most of the coaches seemed to adhere to the guideline. At the outset of our partnership, we asked team members to complete our Through the Eyes of the Team survey to gauge their execution of coaching activities and behaviors. According to their team members, 43 percent of coaches held team meetings on a weekly basis, while another 23 percent held them every other week. Across the organization, only 5 percent of team members reported that their coach never held team meetings.

While team meetings were executed fairly consistently, it was evident that both team members and their coaches struggled with the value of these meetings. According to the team survey, only 15 percent of team members strongly agreed that they found great value in the information provided in team meetings. And in the open-ended comments of the survey, they shared that team meetings were heavy on metrics and company updates but lacked participation from team members and rarely taught them something new.

When we presented these metrics and feedback to the coaches, they admitted that this information was accurate. The coaches didn't look forward to team meetings either. They felt that holding team meetings at least every two weeks was too frequent, and they dreaded having to come up with new, interesting information to share every fourteen days. They agreed that team meetings should be more educational but weren't sure how to do this without creating a huge workload for themselves. Specifically, they were concerned about having to find guest speakers or, even worse, having to create training content and exercises for each team meeting. They were frustrated because they knew they needed to make a change, but they didn't know how to do it.

The first concern to address was the expected frequency of their team meetings. Over two-thirds of the coaches were holding team meetings every other week or weekly. Many of those coaches admitted they were doing this simply to meet expectations, as opposed to finding this frequency helpful to them or their team. You can imagine the relief on their faces when we shared with them that the best frequency for team meetings was actually monthly. They readily agreed that this frequency would be much more beneficial to themselves and their teams. It was a quick, easy adjustment.

The bigger change for our client was to modify its entire approach to team meetings. Like most coaches at the beginning of a consulting relationship with us, these coaches used team meetings primarily

continued

as a way to communicate company updates and performance metrics to team members. The meetings were top-down in their content and were led almost entirely by the coach, with little interaction from the team members. So we recommended a complete overhaul of their typical team meeting agenda as well as sharing responsibility for driving different parts of this agenda.

The goal of the new agenda was to engage team members more in the meeting and to make the content more educational. The coaches added a section to their meeting for team members to take turns sharing best practices with each other. They also designated a portion of the meeting for open discussion of any questions or challenges on which team members wanted their peers' advice. Finally, each coach presented their own development topic during the meeting, ranging from training on a specific skill to discussing an interesting article.

After a few months, we resurveyed their team members to see if team meeting quality had improved. The results were outstanding. Eighty-five percent of team members now agreed or strongly agreed that team meetings were valuable, up 15 percent from the previous survey. Notably, the "top box" score (those who strongly agreed) showed an even greater increase, with 74 percent more team members strongly agreeing that information provided in team meetings was of great value to them.

The coaches were ecstatic. Based on their own observations, the quality of team meetings was improving, so having data to support their opinion was helpful. They shared that their team members were engaging more by asking questions and sharing suggestions. And the new team meeting format was actually easier for them to execute. No longer did they have to organize all the content to be shared each week. Instead, their team members were driving a good portion of the meeting themselves. Plus, a number of them had lowered their team meeting frequency to monthly, so each team meeting felt essential as opposed to required.

IMPROVING YOUR TEAM MEETINGS

As with all the coaching activities we discuss, the quality of your team meetings can be improved by knowing how often they should occur, the right agenda to use, and how to make them more focused on your team's needs. While you may have to experiment to figure out the right formula for you and your team, we have some recommendations that should provide you with a good starting point for improving your team meetings.

Evaluate the frequency of team meetings

The first thing you can do to improve your team meetings is take a critical look at how often you schedule them. When we start working with organizations and ask their team members how often team meetings are conducted, we find that weekly is the most common answer. Most of the time, the reason for holding weekly team meetings is the same—it's what the coaches were told to do by their organizations.

We must confess that we originally thought frequent team meetings were the way to go. When we first started surveying team members, we assumed that the best-performing teams would report that their coaches scheduled their team meetings on a weekly basis. But that is not what the data showed. What we learned is that the coaches who led the highest-performing teams usually held team meetings *less* often than their less effective counterparts. In fact, top-performing coaches were 18 percent more likely than their lower-performing counterparts to hold a team meeting on a monthly basis. And those monthly team meetings were also 13 percent more likely to be rated by team members as providing valuable information than meetings that were held on a weekly basis.

When you are considering the right frequency for your team meetings, think about what you are trying to accomplish with them. We found that the coaches who schedule monthly team meetings are using them primarily to inspire and educate their team members, not as a communication vehicle. If the function of your team requires regular team

WHEN YOU ARE CONSIDERING THE RIGHT FREQUENCY
FOR YOUR TEAM MEETINGS, THINK ABOUT WHAT YOU
ARE TRYING TO ACCOMPLISH WITH THEM.

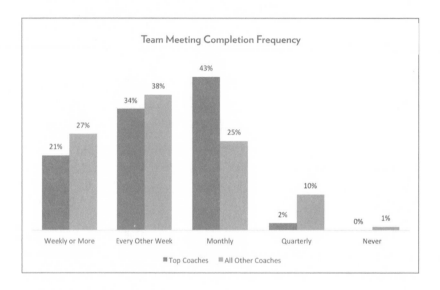

communication or updates, you may want to consider a varied approach
to your team meetings. Perhaps once a month you can make your team
meetings more extensive and educational, and then you can use short,
weekly huddles to update your team members on critical information. As
with all coaching activities, you should always consider the unique needs
of your team and organization.

Review the team meeting agenda

An essential way to improve the quality of your team meetings is to define
an agenda that encourages interaction and information sharing. This doesn't
mean just saving a few minutes at the end of your meeting for questions. It

means having an agenda that proactively drives everyone to ask questions, share ideas, and engage throughout the entirety of the meeting. The key to an interactive team meeting is to define responsibilities for team members. By having specific roles to play during the meeting, they have no choice but to actively engage in what is occurring, and once they have to take an active part in the meeting, they are more likely to continually engage throughout it. In the rest of this chapter, we will share many ideas on what you can do to proactively encourage your team members to engage during team meetings.

The reason for creating a more interactive team meeting agenda is pretty simple: if team members are asked to take a role in the meeting, they enjoy the meeting more and find that it provides information that is more valuable to them. If they know they are going to be asked to contribute during the team meeting, they pay more attention. When team members are given the opportunity to help shape the meeting agenda, they take more ownership in its success. To create this kind of meeting for your team, consider the following best practices in your approach.

START YOUR MEETING BY DISCUSSING PROGRESS TOWARD GOALS

While metrics and data shouldn't be the only focus of a team meeting, it is still important to dedicate some time each meeting to the discussion of company goals, targets, and progress toward them. Ultimately, the performance of your team will be evaluated by how well they accomplish their priorities and help your organization achieve its overall objectives. If you do not include regular updates on the status of your goals, you can lose focus on them.

What you should specifically cover in this portion of the meeting is up to you and how your organization defines success. This is a good time to share any company-wide performance metrics, such as revenue, profit margin, productivity, and quality measurements. You should also have defined performance metrics for your own team that you can share. Your team members should know how they are being measured and whether they are on track with the bigger picture in mind.

The public nature of performance updates can inspire accountability. We like to call this *positive peer pressure*. That is, if your team members are seeing how their peers are contributing and achieving results, they feel more incentive to achieve as well. Simply stated, most people will naturally be more motivated to achieve when they know that those around them are achieving.

This also sets a positive tone for the entire meeting. As you spend the remainder of the meeting sharing best practices, addressing questions, tackling challenges, and recognizing people, you will be doing so with the bigger picture in mind. Your team will naturally consider what's being discussed at your team meeting in the context of progress toward goals.

BEST PRACTICES SHOULD BE SHARED AMONG TEAM MEMBERS

In our surveys, we often receive comments about how team members want to learn more from one another. That makes sense, as our peers are often facing the same challenges we are facing. We want to hear from people who know what we are experiencing and have figured out ways to be successful. We want to know how they've already overcome the same obstacles we are currently facing.

If you've never had best practice sharing as part of your team meeting agenda, it can be challenging at first. Team members who are accustomed to their coach leading the entire meeting may be reluctant to speak up and share their ideas. The easiest way to overcome this challenge is to simply have your team members lead the best practice portion of the meeting.

Having your team members share their best practices at meetings has a few key benefits:

- The person who is assigned to share a best practice has time to prepare how they want to teach their idea.

- The quality of best practice sharing is higher as result of this preparation.

- There is a greater diversity of viewpoints presented because of the increased involvement.

You should give each person on the team a chance to lead the best practice portion of the meeting. If you don't assign responsibility, you will find that the same, more vocal team members keep volunteering at each meeting. You won't get the diversity of ideas you want (which is the goal of this activity), and you may frustrate some of your team members by allowing the loudest voices to dominate the discussion. So assign team members to lead this portion of the meetings, and encourage them to get creative.

There are many different ways your team members can be inventive about sharing best practices with their peers. Some may be comfortable using a slide presentation and a more formal teaching style. Others may just want to share a story of a how they used their best practice with a client. The most important thing is to leave the teaching style up to them. The team will enjoy having different presentation styles. And this variety should make their learning more engaging.

Regardless of how each team member chooses to share their best practice, make sure they make their teaching interactive. Not everyone on your team may be a natural teacher, but they can all ask questions to engage their audience or plan an interactive activity. For example, we've had a team member develop a bingo game with the key points they were sharing about their best practice; the rest of the team would check off these key points on their bingo card as they were mentioned. Keep in mind that you may need to help some of your team members plan for and even rehearse their best practice sharing the first time they do it.

Your team members should be responsible for choosing their own best practice to share. However, you can use your one-to-one meeting time with them to gather ideas. When they share with you a success they had with a client or an innovative approach they took on a project, make a note of it. Then you can remind them of this best practice the next time they are responsible for sharing in a team meeting.

Overall, you can use best practice sharing as a way to not only encourage a diversity of ideas and teaching styles but also to take some of the pressure off of yourself. In traditional team meetings, the coach leads all portions of the meeting and has to determine the content to share. By spreading out the leadership for different portions of team meetings, you can make meetings more engaging and valuable, as well as easier to plan.

In the teams we have personally led, we have seen a change in the camaraderie and team culture as a result of best practice sharing. Over time, your team starts to see how much they can learn from their peers. Naturally, this leads them to look to one another for more advice.

GIVE YOUR TEAM MEMBERS TIME TO SHARE QUESTIONS AND SOLUTIONS

Because we saw team members begin to rely on one another in meetings, we began to encourage coaches to dedicate time in each meeting to discuss how team members find solutions. This portion of the team meeting is essentially open discussion time for your team members to share questions or challenges with which they are struggling. Then, their peers can offer suggestions and solutions based on their experiences. We encourage you to sit back and listen, letting your team support and help one another. This teaches your team that you are not the only person to whom they can turn for advice.

> WE ENCOURAGE YOU TO SIT BACK AND LISTEN, LETTING YOUR TEAM SUPPORT AND HELP ONE ANOTHER.

You will also want to lay some ground rules for this portion of the meeting to ensure the focus stays on solutions, not problems. Let your team know that you encourage discussion of all questions and challenges that would be relevant to the team, but that the focus of the discussion needs to be on what can be done to solve them. This isn't a time for complaining but rather a time for sharing strategies and brainstorming ways to tackle an issue.

While your team members will come to appreciate this open discussion time, they may be reluctant initially to share their challenges with their peers. We all need help at times, but it can be hard for people to admit their struggles to their colleagues. One way to help people feel comfortable talking about challenges is to ask some of your more seasoned team members to take the lead. Once your team sees your best performers asking questions, they will feel better about doing so.

Above all, use this part of the meeting to drive camaraderie among your team members. The more they learn to rely on one another as sounding boards, the more they will reach out to one another, which will increase team cohesion and engagement.

SHARE YOUR OWN DEVELOPMENT TOPIC

While idea sharing is the key to creating engaging team meetings, as the coach you also want to ensure you are providing valuable information. This part of the meeting gives you the opportunity to share any type of information, education, or resources that may help your team members improve their abilities to perform.

You could assign your team an article to read beforehand and then discuss it in the meeting. You could share a story about how your organization positively affected a customer. You could have your team take part in a role-play exercise. You could educate them on a new company product or process. You could ask them to watch a video ahead of time and prepare questions to drive discussion. You could invite someone from another department to be a guest speaker. Essentially, you can share with your team any information, person, exercise, or content that can improve their skills, motivation, or performance.

SHARE WITH YOUR TEAM ANY INFORMATION, PERSON, EXERCISE, OR CONTENT THAT CAN IMPROVE THEIR SKILLS, MOTIVATION, OR PERFORMANCE.

Be creative in deciding what information you want to share with your team. Don't feel like you have to focus only on information that develops specific skills for their roles. Instead, sometimes share content that helps them develop life skills. Have them watch a video on reducing stress. Discuss an article that helps them set personal goals. Invite a speaker who can teach them to manage their time better. While these topics may not be specific to your department, they are certainly relevant to improved performance.

Overall, this is your time to educate and develop your team. Sometimes you may want to share something interesting and fun. Sometimes you may need to educate your team about a policy or process. Whatever the topic may be, in this portion of the meeting, you will be giving your team members information they can use to develop, grow, and improve.

END THE MEETING BY RECOGNIZING SUCCESS

According to our research, one of the most important things a coach can do is recognize and reward their team members. Indeed, our surveys show that 94 percent of team members continue to rate recognition as important regardless of their tenure in the role. Team meetings provide a perfect opportunity to provide this recognition on a consistent basis. This is why we recommend concluding your team meeting with recognition of your team members. It's simply a great way to end your time together on a positive and motivational note.

In our own team meetings, we refer to this part of the agenda as *Cheers for Peers*—a moniker we learned from one of our clients. It's a fun name, but more importantly, it reminds us that recognition should not just be top-down. Sure, we hear from our coaches who want to recognize their team members' successes. But we hear even more from peers who are recognizing each other. Team meetings provide them a great opportunity to publicly thank their colleagues who have helped them out.

You can also consider doing something more inventive to recognize team members during team meetings. Some of our clients have a silly-looking traveling trophy (with an equally silly name) that's given as an award to a different team member at each meeting. Other clients have used written notes for recognition, so the person receiving it not only gets the accolades in the moment but also has something to memorialize it. Another coach gave his team members their favorite candy bar whenever he recognized them. Just a little extra thought put into recognition can help make it more meaningful.

When you are considering the value of recognition, remember that it is not only a way to show appreciation for people's success but also a way to show what you value. When your team members see their peers receiving recognition for their hard work, they learn what is important and valuable to you and their colleagues. In this way, giving recognition, like everything else in a productive team meeting, can become an effective way to teach your team members.

RELY ON AND LOOK FORWARD TO TEAM MEETINGS

Team meetings present a great opportunity to build camaraderie, communication, and education for your team. However, these meetings must be done well in order to have the desired impact. It's important to remember that *how* information is discussed and presented is as important as *what* information is discussed and presented. If you drive interaction, conversation, and shared ideas during team meetings, your team members will see them as one of the best parts of being on your team.

*A Team Meeting template can be found at www.ecsellinstitute.com/templates

#WhatTeamMembersSay

> "His weekly meetings are insightful and include a ton of good information sharing. They always have a clear, productive agenda. I love when he brings in experts to train us and allows us to ask questions."

—Through the Eyes of the Team survey respondent

6

Performance Feedback

#WhatTeamMembersSay

"When giving feedback, he should guide the employee toward possible solutions as opposed to testing them on new information before it has been shared with the employee. This creates a tense working environment and is very discouraging to new hires."

—Through the Eyes of the Team survey respondent

RECENTLY, ONE OF THE coaches at a client organization communicated to us that he was struggling with giving feedback to a team member. The coach was particularly close to this team member—they had been friends for years and even spent time together on the weekends with their families. Unfortunately, this team member was having some significant performance issues, and the coach was having a hard time finding the courage to address it. He didn't want to hurt his team member's feelings. He didn't want to have what he knew would be an awkward conversation because of their closeness. And he especially didn't want to do anything that could damage his friendship with this person.

Like many of us, this coach wasn't looking at feedback the right way. He was focused on how he would feel delivering it, rather than how his team member may feel about receiving it. When we are teaching coaches how to deliver constructive feedback, we often liken it to telling someone that they have a piece of spinach in their teeth. If you had a piece of spinach stuck in your teeth, wouldn't you want to know? Aren't you usually appreciative that the friend mentioned it to you, instead of letting you walk around all day smiling at people with a green glob stuck between your teeth? Performance feedback works the same way.

GOOD FEEDBACK IS A GIFT

Good feedback is a gift to the people receiving it. It helps them improve their skills. It helps them overcome challenges. It helps them achieve their performance goals. And, yes, it even helps them avoid the embarrassment of making a mistake that everyone but they can see.

In fact, when we look at the different coaching activities executed by the coaches of our client organizations, we see that delivering effective, consistent, and documented feedback is one of the biggest factors in driving team performance. In a recent study we completed for one of our clients, the coaches who led the best-performing teams, as measured by each team's percent to sales goal, completed over double the amount of documented feedback conversations as the coaches who led lower-performing teams. This finding is not unique, and we've seen it replicated in many of our client organizations over the years. Simply stated, giving consistent, effective feedback has a high relationship to improved team performance.

The impact of feedback on performance is really not that surprising. As a coach, when you help your team members understand what they're doing well, what they're doing poorly, and what they can do to improve, they have the information they need to get better. Sounds simple, right? Then why aren't more coaches giving consistent, effective feedback to improve their team's performance? Why doesn't everyone make this a key priority on their to-do list? Unfortunately, many coaches simply don't know how to give good feedback.

A Coaching Success Story

A couple of years ago, we were working with a newly formed sales leadership team at a consumer products company. Although everyone on the leadership team had a long tenure with the company, most of them had been newly promoted to a leadership role. Their vice president of sales hired us to teach these new coaches how to lead their teams effectively.

We took our typical approach and began teaching the coaches the basics of how to conduct different coaching activities with their teams. What became apparent over the following months is that one coaching activity was proving particularly difficult for the team—delivering feedback on their team members' skills.

Some of the coaches struggled to find the right balance between being direct in their feedback while also being careful not to make their team members feel defensive. They fell short in giving feedback that was specific enough to help their team members change behavior. They also found it difficult to take the time to give feedback consistently. And there was one coach in particular, Jenny, who found improving her feedback to be a big challenge.

Jenny was a newly promoted coach who had excelled as an individual performer in her organization. She was energetic, driven, and smart, and she had always delivered on her sales goals. She was exactly the type of team member most of us hope to hire. When she was promoted to a coaching role, she expected her success to continue unabated. What she found was that success in coaching required a completely different skill set.

continued

Jenny's greatest challenge was providing feedback to her team members on how to improve their customer skills. Jenny was a perfectionist who liked her team to complete their work the way that she would. Even though she had good intentions around driving accountability, her coaching style led to her micromanaging every detail.

When it came to feedback, only a little over half of her team felt like she was effective in giving them the kind of information and ideas that helped them improve their skills. Most of them agreed that she did not include them in important decisions. And less than a third of her team felt comfortable expressing their opinions when they disagreed with her.

In short, Jenny's team felt like she had an aggressive coaching style in which she was more focused on telling them how to do their jobs than collaborating with them to improve their skills.

Jenny took this feedback to heart and made a concerted effort to change her coaching style. She worked with us to define the areas where she needed the most improvement. After a couple of conversations, Jenny decided to focus on how she engaged with her team when giving them direction and feedback on their work. Following our recommendations, she stopped overprescribing to her team members how they needed to execute their responsibilities. Instead, she started asking them questions to help them figure out the right approach themselves.

She also learned to change her approach when dealing with a performance issue. Previously, she had been extremely tactical in defining the actions her team members needed to take to improve. Instead, she figured out how to drive more responsibility for making improvement to her team members. She'd ask them to define the follow-up actions they needed to take for themselves. She offered her thoughts and feedback on their plans but didn't force them to implement her ideas. She let them figure out strategies on their own, and she even let them make some mistakes if those mistakes could help them learn. In short, she went from being a manager of details to being a supportive coach.

This shift in coaching style paid significant dividends for Jenny and her team. A few months later, when we surveyed her team again, they specifically noted how effective her feedback had become. As they praised her for giving them guidance on how they could improve their weaknesses, they also noted how well she listened to them and their ideas. Most importantly, Jenny's team had improved by 7 percent in achieving their sales goals in just six months.

Like Jenny, many coaches don't know how to deliver effective feedback. Some are too aggressive and leave their team members feeling demoralized by the end of the conversation. Some coaches are not direct, and their team members are confused about where they need to improve. Some give recommendations that are too general, so their team members don't know how to change their behavior. And some simply don't want to take the time for feedback, so they quickly tell their team members what to do rather than engaging in a conversation to help them learn how to work differently. If a coach wants their team members to improve their performance, the coach must first improve their feedback.

> IF A COACH WANTS THEIR TEAM MEMBERS TO IMPROVE THEIR PERFORMANCE, THE COACH MUST FIRST IMPROVE THEIR FEEDBACK.

Dr. Peter Jensen is one of the best thought leaders on delivering effective feedback. Dr. Jensen is the founder of Performance Coaching and an instructor at Canada's elite business school, Queen's University Smith School of Business. But Dr. Jensen is not just an academic. He has also worked with the Canadian Olympic team for years as a sports psychologist. Despite his busy schedule, we have been lucky enough to have Dr. Jensen speak at many of our coaching summits.

Above all, he has been a generous friend by always making time to share his insights on coaching with us.

As a coach who has worked with more than forty Olympic medal winners, Dr. Jensen knows that the best coaches are the ones who can develop people to realize their full potential. "In the end, it's all about people—and the relationship between the leader and his or her player," Dr. Jensen says.[3] Dr. Jensen's wisdom about what drives the performance of world-class athletes and the coaches who guide them offers numerous insights that we can apply in a professional setting.

For Dr. Jensen, effective coaching always begins with the creation of a trusting relationship between the coach and the person they are coaching. This means you must first understand your team member before you can help them improve. What makes them tick? What's their decision process? How do they learn best? You won't know unless you get to know them better. And this is best accomplished by asking your team member questions and actively listening to their responses.

For many coaches, it can be hard to ask questions and listen rather than tell someone what they need to do differently. After all, most coaches were promoted into a management role because they had good ideas and an ability to execute them. But when you are the one talking, you are not helping your team members learn how to think differently. Active listening requires you to not just nod your head while you are distracted with other things. It means putting down your mobile phone, ignoring your email alerts, and giving your undivided attention to your team member. As Dr. Jensen notes, "active listening has the benefit of improving our trust relationship with our team members, as we are showing that we value what they have to say."[4]

Delivering effective feedback is another way you can increase your trust relationship with your team members. When you give feedback, you are sharing your time, ideas, and support because you want them to be

---

3   Peter Jensen, *Ignite the Third Factor* (Ontario: Thomas Allen & Son, 2011).

4   Jensen, *Ignite*.

> DELIVERING EFFECTIVE FEEDBACK IS ANOTHER WAY YOU CAN INCREASE YOUR TRUST RELATIONSHIP WITH YOUR TEAM MEMBERS.

successful. As stated earlier, good feedback can truly be a gift to the person receiving it. Learning to deliver this type of meaningful, growth-oriented feedback is one of the most important things a successful coach can do.

IMPROVING YOUR FEEDBACK

Learning to give great feedback is a lifelong learning experience for most coaches, as it's one of the most challenging coaching skills to master. Not only do you have to be able to clearly articulate the points you want to make but you also have to ensure that you create an effective back-and-forth with the person to whom you are giving feedback. Most importantly, you have to really understand your team members so you know when to be more direct, when to be positive, and when to challenge them into Complexity. The strategies that follow should help you continue refining your approach to feedback as you determine the best way to give it to each of your team members.

Pay attention to frequency and tone

Regular feedback should be the norm, not the exception. Think back to before you were a coach, when you were an individual performer. How much feedback were you given, and how often did you receive it? Was it immediate or delayed? Did your coach give feedback on a regular basis or mostly when you made a mistake? If you are like most people, chances are you didn't receive feedback that often, and when you did, it was because you messed something up.

If our goal is to make feedback a positive experience, we can't just give it when something goes wrong. By doing so, we create a negative, almost Pavlovian response in our team members. That is, as soon as we begin to give them feedback, they immediately assume it's because they've done something wrong. Is it any wonder why some team members dread receiving feedback from their coaches?

Regularity in feedback helps team members accept it and view it in a positive light. Over time, feedback just becomes part of the workflow, because it's given when we succeed *and* when we fail. It's simply something we always give and receive because we want to improve and we want to help others improve. More consistent feedback also has the added benefit of ensuring that feedback is timelier. That is, if a coach is giving feedback all the time, then they are much more likely to provide feedback soon after the performance has occurred.

Provide timely feedback

Feedback that is given shortly after performance rather than delayed helps the team member make changes in their processes more readily, and it helps them understand the need for the feedback being given. The memory is still fresh, so specific details about the event are readily recalled. On the other hand, delayed feedback hinders the growth process because of forgetfulness. When the work or task being evaluated happened months ago, there will likely be confusion about what exactly went right or wrong.

There's not a surefire frequency at which feedback should be provided, but it's apparent that most team members do not feel like they receive enough of it. According to our Through the Eyes of the Team surveys, 31 percent of team members say they receive feedback from their coaches never or rarely.

Furthermore, our surveys indicate that 87 percent of team members actually prefer more frequent, smaller doses of feedback to less frequent, more formal feedback. Knowing this, we recommend to our clients that coaches provide verbal feedback to their team members at a minimum frequency of monthly, with more in-depth documented feedback occurring on at least a quarterly basis. To reiterate, this is just a minimum expectation, and we encourage you to provide feedback more frequently to your team members if they need it. We've heard many complaints from team members who don't feel like they receive feedback often enough but few complaints that they receive too much. If you are going to err, err on the side of more frequent feedback.

Of course, regularity in feedback alone doesn't guarantee an effective feedback process. A coach can give a lot of feedback, but if it lacks substance, it will not yield the intended value. One of the ways we encourage our clients to create feedback conversations of more depth is by using a simple format for delivering it. With a little bit more structure, the coach is more likely to review the important skills their team members need to possess and, most importantly, to deliver feedback that is specific enough to be acted on.

Be clear and specific

When we ask team members how feedback from their coaches could be improved, the most common responses indicate a desire for it to be clearer and more specific. Too often, the coaches' comments are general, and team members don't walk away with a clear sense of what exactly they need to do differently. Indeed, our surveys clearly indicate that only about 25 percent of team members "strongly agree" that their coach's feedback provides them with the help and knowledge they need to improve their performance. So make sure the feedback you give your team members is full of actionable advice.

FEEDBACK NEEDS STRUCTURE

Even though team members may prefer more informal feedback because it can be delivered more frequently, sometimes more depth is needed to help the team member improve. This is where a structure for feedback (specifically, using a documented process for delivering it) can be helpful to the coach. Taking the time to document feedback and then reviewing that documentation with your team member is helpful for several reasons:

- It reduces ambiguity—both coach and team member are seeing the same information.

- It improves learning—documentation can be referred back to in the days and weeks to come.

- It is more comprehensive—more essential skills are listed and evaluated.

- It encourages specific improvement ideas—documenting drives us to be more precise.

- It shows progress over time—team members can look back to see how they've improved.

- It focuses the feedback—coaches don't get sidetracked on less important discussions.

Unfortunately, we learned through our surveys that half of team members receive documented feedback on their skills only once per year, despite the importance of effective feedback. Worse yet, 20 percent of team members reported they never receive any kind of documented feedback from their coach. It's no wonder that many team members find feedback to be insufficient in providing them with ideas for what they can do to improve.

Identify necessary skills

To create an effective feedback form for your team members, you must first identify the significant skills and attributes a team member needs to possess to be successful in their role. Focus on behaviors or skills that most

> YOU WANT TO PROVIDE YOUR TEAM MEMBERS WITH CONSTRUCTIVE FEEDBACK ON THINGS THEY CAN ACTUALLY CHANGE AND IMPROVE.

team members can develop, such as building good client relationships, as opposed to personality traits that may be more innate, such as being extroverted. You want to provide your team members with constructive feedback on things they can actually change and improve.

Although the list of skills needs to be comprehensive, it shouldn't be too long or detailed because you don't want to overwhelm your team member with too much information. An evaluation list consisting of seven to twelve key skills is more than adequate to do a proper evaluation. Also, even though you may evaluate a number of skills on a feedback form, offer detailed improvement ideas on only two or three of them. Your team members can't improve everything at once, and too much feedback can make anyone feel overwhelmed. They will be more likely to take action on two to three detailed, specific suggestions than a dozen general thoughts.

Rate skills when appropriate

Rating skills numerically can be a useful tool when giving performance feedback, but whether you should use this tool is not set in stone. In general, we believe that rating skills is a good way to create more clarity about your team members' skill levels. Even when feedback is documented, team members can sometimes walk away with a skewed perception about what their coach meant. Numerical ratings come with the benefit of a higher level of clarity. Numerical ratings can also be useful in giving team members a clear sense of their progress over time. When a team member's skill in an area was rated a 2 on their feedback form two months ago and it's now rated a 4, they will clearly see their growth and feel a sense of accomplishment.

On the other hand, numerical ratings can be a distraction in some feed-back conversations. That is, the team member receiving feedback can get so focused on the number and whether they agree with it that they miss out on the important insights their coach is sharing. We encourage you to use your judgment to determine if you want to include skill ratings on your feedback form. Overall, we feel the value of ratings usually outweighs the potential downside.

EFFECTIVE FEEDBACK TECHNIQUES

Having a defined frequency and format for delivering feedback increases the coach's ability to have an effective feedback conversation. However, the most important element of good feedback is how the coach actually delivers it. You can have numerous valuable insights to share, but if your delivery style makes your team member feel defensive, overwhelmed, or confused, you will not have presented them with any information of value. In fact, they may feel less certain of how to improve than before you had a conversation with them.

Dr. Peter Jensen lists Four Rules of Feedback that offer good guidance on how to facilitate an effective conversation with your team members.

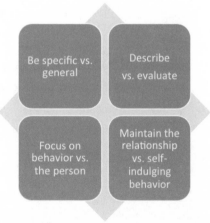

Be specific rather than general

As we shared previously, one of the biggest complaints we see on our team surveys is that feedback is too general and does little to help the team member getting the feedback realize where they need to improve. Imagine if a golf instructor were to simply tell their student that they need to hit the ball farther. That would add zero value. Yet, sometimes when we give feedback, we use that same kind of generic language. We tell people to be more assertive or more strategic, without discussing ideas on exactly how they can change their behavior. So rather than telling our team member to get to know their client better, we should share some specific questions they could ask to deepen the client relationship. Rather than just suggesting they improve their time management, we should review their current priorities with them and help them plan how to spend their time. As a general rule of thumb, your team member should be able to clearly visualize how they should change their approach in order to achieve the desired result. If they can't get a picture in their mind of how their actions should look different, the feedback conversation probably hasn't led to suggestions that are specific enough.

Describe their behavior rather than evaluate it

The quickest way to put a team member on the defensive when giving feedback is to place judgment on their performance. If you tell them they did something wrong or poorly or make a similar type of judgment, their mind is likely to quickly go to defending their actions rather than listening to your feedback. Try to stick to describing what you saw them do in a fact-based way. For example, rather than saying, "Your strategy doesn't seem well thought out," instead say, "As I read your strategy, I noticed it didn't contain certain elements." If you are just describing what you saw or heard, it's harder for them to take issue with your account. Once you are both on the same page about their actions and behaviors, then you can work together to try to figure out a different approach they can take next time they are presented with a similar situation. This allows the feedback conversation to feel much more collaborative.

Focus on behavior rather than the person

One of the most difficult aspects of delivering effective feedback is helping the person you are coaching feel like they can actually improve. Simply put, change is hard; you want to make sure your team member leaves a feedback conversation feeling like they can actually apply the feedback to get a better result. By focusing on their behavior rather than who they are as a person, you send the messages that it's simply their actions that need to be different and that they don't have to change their personality to be more effective.

As an example, instead of telling a team member who works in customer service that they need to be a "more helpful person" or that they should "care more about customers," you can coach them to follow a new process for dealing with customer complaints. It's easier for them to feel like they can change a current approach or behavior rather than who they are.

Maintain the relationship rather than self-indulging

We are coaches, but we are also human. That means at times we may be thinking about or focusing on ourselves, rather than the team member we are coaching, when giving feedback. It's fun to share our experiences, and it feels good to show off our knowledge. But when we are more focused on proving to our team members how smart we are, we are not focused on helping them learn and improve. If you tend to be a talker and a storyteller, before giving feedback remind yourself to keep the focus on the other person, their behaviors, their experiences, and how they can develop and grow. They will appreciate you giving them smart feedback on how to improve more than you just being smart.

QUESTIONS: THE SECRET WEAPON OF EFFECTIVE FEEDBACK

If we could offer only one piece of advice to coaches who want to improve their feedback, it would be to ask more questions. This can be a lot harder than it sounds. Like most coaches, you were likely promoted to your role because you were successful in the role that you are now coaching others to do. When you are good at something, it can be difficult to sit back and listen. You have valuable experiences. You have helpful insights. You have good ideas. And most of all, you have solutions that could help your team members achieve their goal if they'd just listen to you. It's important, though, to realize that you can perhaps offer them the most help by first listening to them.

> IF WE COULD OFFER ONLY ONE PIECE OF ADVICE TO COACHES WHO WANT TO IMPROVE THEIR FEEDBACK, IT WOULD BE TO ASK MORE QUESTIONS.

Questions increase engagement

In their desire to help their team members, most coaches are quick to give advice and often spend feedback conversations doing most of the talking. Unfortunately, the coaches' greatest thoughts often get lost in all the talking they do. Because when coaches talk and talk and talk, it is harder for their team members to take in their ideas. This is because most people are not passive learners. It's difficult for people to be able to decipher a lesson when they are being talked at and then take that advice and apply it. People tend to learn better when they are engaging in the conversation. And there's no better way to help someone engage than to ask them questions.

We have an exercise we like to do with coaches in our seminars. We have them simulate a feedback conversation with a partner, with one person playing the coach and the other person playing the team member receiving feedback. We only give one ground rule for this conversation—the coach cannot give any feedback, advice, or suggestions until they've asked at least seven questions.

Questions increase collaboration

When we debrief the exercise, the coaches all admit how hard it is to ask so many questions before giving feedback. Many of them want to jump in with their ideas immediately after asking their first question. Others are more comfortable getting out a few questions before the itch to talk really kicks in.

Yet, in spite of their discomfort with this new approach, the coaches always recognize that the simulated feedback conversation goes much better than their typical feedback. They like how their partner shares more insights. They feel like the other person actually self-identifies issues and strategies for addressing them quite often. And the people playing the team member always remark how the conversation feels collaborative. They even say they don't feel like they were being coached, but rather that they are just talking with someone about ways to get a better result.

Questions promote self-discovery

One of the major benefits of questions is that they promote self-discovery. By asking your team members questions, you are helping them learn how to evaluate their own performance. This allows them to self-identify the areas where they feel they can improve. Ultimately this will also help them make necessary changes, because when people recognize themselves that they need to get better, they are much more likely to be open to suggestions.

Be mindful of tone

Keep in mind that using questions to coach can be problematic when you do it the wrong way. When asking questions, be sure to watch your tone of voice. If you tend to be a very direct or matter-of-fact communicator, your questions could be perceived as aggressive. You don't want to put people on the defensive, so be careful not to make your questions seem like a cross-examination in which you are trying to get the other person to slip up.

One of the best ways to ensure that your questions don't feel too aggressive is to ask more *what* questions and fewer *why* questions. Asking someone why they did something can often make them feel like you disagree with their judgment and therefore put them on the defensive. Instead, ask your team members what they wanted to accomplish with their approach. Ask them what they learned from completing the task. Ask them what they'd like to try differently next time.

Above all, use questions as a way to learn more about your team members—how they think, how they want to improve, and how you can help them. The more you ask questions when giving feedback, the more likely you are to learn what you can do to be a better coach to them.

USE FEEDBACK TO DRIVE GROWTH

When we study the best coaches, we find that the ability to deliver effective feedback is one of the most crucial skills they can possess. This is because by giving good feedback, they are essentially facilitating a learning experience for someone else. And the only way people can actually improve is to first learn a new or different way from what they are currently doing.

At times, this can create a feeling of discomfort in the team member who is receiving feedback. When you are helping your team member realize that there is something they don't know or a skill they haven't mastered, they may recoil somewhat. For many people, it can be unsettling to admit to their coach that they're not great at something. But that's why giving feedback is so essential. It's an intentional experience to move our team members outside their comfort zones and into Complexity.

We've discussed in depth the value of putting your team in a state of Complexity. Effective feedback conversations are one of the most useful ways to do this. Indeed, we often see a strong relationship in our survey data between coaches who are highly rated as driving Complexity and coaches who are also highly rated in giving effective feedback.

As a coach who is trying to help others grow, challenge yourself to create at least one aha moment every time you give feedback. Your team members should always leave a feedback conversation with valuable information they didn't have when they began it: they should have learned something about themselves or their work; they should have a new idea or strategy they want to try. This is what makes your feedback truly a gift to your team.

*A Performance Feedback template can be found at www.ecsellinstitute. com/templates

#WhatTeamMembersSay

"She is incredibly supportive in all aspects of my life. She doesn't scold me if I do something wrong, but instead coaches and helps me to understand why and how to improve. She really harnesses my strengths and helps me excel at them."

—*Through the Eyes of the Team survey respondent*

7

Career Development

"My manager is only looking out for himself. He does not do any real coaching that is productive or that we need to be successful. He only cares about the end result to affect his numbers and not at all about the development of his team members."

—*Through the Eyes of the Team survey respondent*

SUPPORTING AND GUIDING YOUR team members in developing their careers is one of the most important yet most challenging things you can do as a coach. Using our Through the Eyes of the Team surveys, we studied the coaching activities and behaviors that drove team member success, and our research revealed that having a coach who helped team members make progress toward their long-term career-development goals strongly increased that person's achievement of their current daily work goals. That is, investment in a person's long-term growth also yielded short-term performance benefits. Yet when we asked these same team members how effective their coaches were in doing this, career development ranked among the lowest-rated skill sets that their coaches possessed. It's a vital activity, but it is also a difficult one.

MAKE CAREER DEVELOPMENT A PRIORITY

For many coaches, and for their team members, career development simply feels optional. There are so many critical priorities to accomplish on a day-to-day basis that it's easy to move longer-term career development to the back burner. But the top-performing coaches we have studied recognize the importance of career development and make it a priority for their teams as well.

A Coaching Success Story

One coach who has learned the importance of career development is Becky, a sales team coach at a large, publicly traded organization. Becky has worked in her industry for decades and has a long track record of success, both as an individual performer and as the coach of a team. When our coaching program was instituted at Becky's organization, we learned through our Through the Eyes of the Team surveys that she was already regarded as an excellent coach by 75 percent of her team. In addition, 100 percent of her team members agreed that she cared about them as people, not just as employees. And her good coaching was reflected in tangible results—Becky's team consistently achieved their sales goals.

However, one area where Becky struggled was ensuring that her team members were being challenged to constantly improve and grow their long-term skills. Only 13 percent of Becky's team members strongly agreed that she purposely asked them to do things that stretched their abilities. Similarly, only 13 percent rated her ability to help them achieve their career goals as very strong. Becky was a good coach of day-to-day work, but not necessarily one that pushed her team to develop their skills to ensure their longer-term career growth.

When we introduced our career-development plan coaching activity to her organization, Becky immediately began using it with her team. Although the coaches at Becky's company were given months by their leadership to complete career-development discussions, Becky scheduled all of her discussions with her team members immediately. Knowing this was an area where her coaching was lacking according to her team surveys, she intentionally made it a high priority.

Over the next few weeks, Becky held career discussions with each of her team members. Using the career-development questions that we had helped her organization define, she asked her team members about their personal and professional goals. She asked which of their talents were currently being underutilized. She asked about their interests and motivations. She asked how they liked to be recognized. Most importantly, she asked how they'd like to grow and develop and how she could help them. Becky admitted to us that she was surprised at how little she had known about her team's developmental interests and long-term goals prior to having these conversations.

After conducting all of her career-development discussions with her team, Becky asked each of them to define one or two strategies they wanted to pursue over the next year to work toward their long-term career goals. Then, she partnered with them to define specific tactics they'd pursue and timelines for completing them. As their coach, she also defined the specific steps she was going to take to support their plans and, importantly, to help hold them accountable.

Because of Becky's actions, her team began proactively pursuing development opportunities immediately, and this paid off for her team in a significant way a few months later. Becky's organization instituted a program to encourage team members to advance and grow their

continued

skill sets outside of their daily responsibilities. As part of this program, team members who could show how they had pursued development opportunities and proactively advanced their skills could qualify for a bump in both their compensation and title. As soon as the program was introduced, all of Becky's team members immediately qualified for these increases.

Needless to say, Becky was thrilled for her team and proud of how her proactive investment in their career development had helped them achieve their goals. Becky's team was excited too. The next time they assessed Becky in our Through the Eyes of the Team survey, 100 percent of them reported they had a career discussion with Becky within the past year and 100 percent strongly agreed that Becky had helped them progress toward their career objectives. Becky's team also flourished in their regular responsibilities during this time period, as they achieved 122 percent of their sales target for the year.

The kind of results that Becky was able to achieve in helping her team progress toward their long-term career objectives, as well as exceed performance expectations in their current role, is not an anomaly. Indeed, our research shows a strong statistical relationship between team members who rate their coaches as "very strong" in helping them with their career development and higher levels of motivation to succeed in their current role. Team members who are learning and growing, and who also have the support of their coach in doing so, simply are more engaged in their work.

Unfortunately, our Through the Eyes of the Team survey indicates that one-third of team members have not had any kind of career-development discussion with their coach in the past year. That means one out of every three team members are not even being asked about how they'd like to grow in their career, let alone working with their coach to create a plan for their development.

Let's face it: if a salesperson is hitting their sales number, nobody will care if they aren't investing in the development of their skills to achieve their long-term objectives. If a customer service professional has high satisfaction ratings from their clients and is effective at retaining them, their company will not care if they aren't pushing themselves to take on new challenges. Career development is like saving for your future, but the people around you want your money now. This is why the best coaches are often the ones pushing their team members to keep growing, even when their team members are not focused on it.

> THE BEST COACHES ARE OFTEN THE ONES PUSHING THEIR TEAM MEMBERS TO KEEP GROWING.

Ultimately, helping your team members develop their career is worth it. And it's not just because it's the right thing to do; it's because the data shows that career development yields better outcomes in terms of performance. Team members who rate their coaches as effective at helping them reach their career goals are 27 percent more likely to be effective at achieving their individual goals. They are more engaged not only in their long-term objectives but also in their current role, reporting a 31 percent higher level of motivation to perform.

CAREER DEVELOPMENT SHOULD BE HIGHLY INDIVIDUALIZED

If helping team members make progress toward their career goals drives motivation to perform in their current role and improves long-term skills development, why isn't every coach making career development a priority? When we have asked this question of coaches, the most common reason they give for not having career discussions is that they don't know how to respond to the career goals that their team members may share. This is because many coaches, and many organizations for that matter, conflate career development with promotional opportunities. To them, helping somebody reach their career goals means helping them move into a management role, but most times this is not the case.

For most team members, management is not the right path. Certainly, some people on your team may be interested in filling your shoes someday. But when we talk to coaches who actually ask their team members about their career goals, most admit that their team members want to stay in their individual-performer roles. The reasons for this vary. Some people have no interest in the stresses and headaches that can come along with a management role. Others simply don't find the responsibilities of management to be appealing. Still others feel like they don't have the right talent to be a coach or a leader of a team. In general, the message is clear—the majority of people who report to you probably don't want your job.

So career development can't really be about setting up your team member for a promotion to management. Instead, you, your team, and your organization must think of career development as a way to help people grow and develop their skills and experiences for whatever their current and future goals may be. In this way, effective career development is all about a person's unique goals, talents, and interests. Simply put, it is highly individualized.

This is also why you can't rely on a career-development program from your organization to fill the gap in helping your team members develop. First, most companies do not have any type of formal career-development opportunities. Second, the few that do tend to simply offer workshops to educate on a specific job-related skill, as opposed to offering hands-on experiences that will help your team truly acquire and apply abilities that help them prepare for their long-term priorities. Third, company development programs are not highly individualized, which makes their impact less relevant to each person's unique aspirations.

Taken together, these challenges make career development very difficult for coaches to drive. You have to take the time to get to know your team members and truly understand their talents, goals, and areas of interests. Then, you have to work with them to identify experiences that will help them develop in their desired areas. Finally, and most importantly, you have to drive accountability for career development with them. With these challenges, it's easy to see why many coaches, team members, and organizations do not make career development a priority.

HAVING A CAREER-DEVELOPMENT DISCUSSION

The first step in helping your team members create a plan for their career development is to have a discussion with them about their goals and how they hope to grow. Because effective career development has to be highly individualized to the person, you can't just put somebody into a company development program and expect them to flourish. As their coach, you have to first figure out how they want to grow and how you can support them. At EcSell, we recommend following certain guidelines when approaching these discussions.

Before the discussion

An important part of having an effective career discussion is doing the right preparation. Simple steps like determining the right frequency for your discussions, knowing the questions you will ask, and sharing those questions with your team members ahead of the discussion can greatly increase the discussion's effectiveness.

DETERMINE THE FREQUENCY OF DISCUSSION

We recommend that coaches hold a career discussion with each of their team members on at least an annual basis. People's needs, goals, interests, and skills change regularly, so if you are not touching base with your team members about their career goals at least annually, you are likely missing out on developments and changes that could help you support them more effectively.

Since career discussions are only held annually, don't be surprised if they last up to two hours. An important aspect of holding these discussions is getting to know your team members better, so trying to squeeze them into a short time period would certainly send the wrong message. Also, you want to make sure you leave yourself time to ask additional follow-up questions. Your pre-written questions are only intended to be a guide for the discussion, and they will likely need to change as new information is revealed.

MAP OUT YOUR DISCUSSION

The questions you ask your team members are some of the most important aspects of an effective career discussion. Too often team members are asked generic questions such as, "Where do you see yourself in five years?" Overly broad questions like this can be difficult for people to answer unless they've already thought about their career goals and have identified specific priorities they have to achieve them. And remember, as shown by our Through the Eyes of the Team surveys, many team members are not asked to think about and plan for their career goals on a regular basis. So if they haven't taken the initiative themselves, they may have no idea of where they'd like to be in five months, let alone five years.

If you want to help your team members start to identify their longer-term career goals, you need to have specific questions that spark their imagination. Questions that make them think about their interests, their unique skills, and what they love about their work can help them identify developmental opportunities they may want to pursue. As their coach, your goal is to ask them questions that get them thinking about things they rarely think about.

We recommend career discussion questions that focus on three areas:

1. **Overall goals and needs**—First and foremost, you need to have a deeper understanding of your team members as people. What motivates them? How do they like to be recognized? What do they see as their greatest areas of strength? What personal goals do they have? When a team member shares this kind of information with you, they are sharing insights that can help you better understand them as a person so you can coach to their unique needs and abilities.

2. **Current role goals and needs**—Asking about your team members' goals and needs in their current roles is one of the most important aspects of a career discussion. As we shared earlier, most of your team members are unlikely to have the desire or skills to move into a management position someday, so talking about ways that they can continue to develop as an individual performer is essential. In this area, you will also want to ask about the support and motivation they need to reach those goals and how they can leverage their talents more effectively.

3. **Potential future roles**—Although most of your team members may have no desire to change roles, some will be interested in management or simply a different type of individual-performer position someday. If moving into leadership or a different role is a team member's goal, it is important for you to know this so you can help them determine the right path. First, you will want to ask questions to help your team member determine if the role they're considering truly fits their talents and interests and, if so, how they can begin to prepare themselves for it. Conversely, if a different role is not the right fit for the team member, you can help them determine a different future direction that fits them best.

Engaging, open-ended questions focused on these areas can help create an effective dialogue between you and your team member. Here are some of the specific questions we recommend to our clients:

- What are your passions and motivations?

- List your greatest talents and skills that should be utilized in your role.

- What is the most effective way for you to set goals? How can I assist you in setting them?

- What personal life goals do you wish to share?

- What do you get paid to do?

- What specifically would like to accomplish this next year?

- What obstacles could prevent you from achieving your goal?

- What skills do you need to further develop that would allow you to achieve that goal?

- What other professional skills would you like to enhance or learn?

- Are there certain people or departments with whom you would like to work more closely?

- Define success within your current role.

- Do you have a passion or goal to teach or develop others?

- What areas of interest should we consider as we watch your career develop?

- As you see things today, what are your professional aspirations?

- Please explain the role you would like me to play in helping you accomplish your goals.

- When you achieve your goals, how would you like to be recognized?

Once you've selected your career-development discussion questions, we recommend that you send these questions to your team members a few days in advance of your conversation. We've all had goal discussions in which people don't really know what to say because they haven't thought much about their goals before. You don't want that to happen in your career discussions with your team, so give them time to consider your questions and their responses ahead of your meeting. The meeting will be much more productive if everyone is prepared.

In addition, we encourage you to ask your team members to write down their thoughts on the questions you sent. Their responses don't have to be elaborate—short sentences or bullet points are sufficient. But they should write down their thoughts and share them with you before your discussion. This will help ensure you are prepared to respond effectively to the ideas and goals they express.

If you don't have any idea of what they will say, you could be left in an awkward position when they ask for your help on something you weren't expecting. For example, a team member could catch you off guard if they say they want to be a manager and you see their talents as suiting an individual performer. How would you tactfully handle this in the moment? Or maybe they express an idea for which they need a considerable investment of your time. Is this an investment you're willing to make without time to think through the ramifications?

Overall, having specific questions that stimulate your team member's thinking and allowing time for preparation for both of you is likely to produce a discussion that is much more effective in helping them reach their goals.

Sarah's Development Story

When I speak of the impact that can be created by a career-development discussion, I speak from personal experience—this book is a result of a career discussion between Bill and me. A few years ago, Bill and I were having our annual career-development discussion. He was asking me all of the questions that we just recommended to you, and we were having

continued

a good dialogue about different ways I could grow in my current role. When we got to the question on my professional aspirations, I don't remember the answer I shared with Bill, but I specifically remember his response. He said to me, "I want you to dream bigger." Whatever aspiration I had shared with Bill, he clearly believed I was capable of more and he challenged me to articulate what I really wanted. So I took a moment and finally admitted, "I want to write a book someday." If Bill was surprised or skeptical, he didn't show it. Instead, he simply replied, "I didn't know that. Let's see if we can make that happen someday." A couple of years went by as we were busy building our business, but Bill would bring up my aspiration from time to time. Finally, in early 2016, we decided to try in earnest to make this goal a reality and submitted a book proposal to a few publishers. I'll never forget the excitement on Bill's face when he told me that our book proposal had been accepted and my dream was coming true.

During the discussion

The next step is to conduct the career discussion with your team member. During the discussion, your role is to ask your pre-planned questions, listen intently, then help your team member determine their goals. Since you had the opportunity to review their responses ahead of the meeting, you should be well prepared to help them identify specific goals or opportunities they'd like to pursue to develop their careers. Ultimately, you want to help them determine what to include in a short, specific career-development plan.

CREATE A CAREER-DEVELOPMENT PLAN

During the discussion, your goal is to work with your team member to identify at least one, but no more than three, priorities they'd like to pursue over the next year to develop their career. Although numerous ideas will likely come up in the course of your conversation, you want to help them focus on the ideas that are most important to achieving their goals. Pursuing too many development priorities at once makes it less likely that they will be able to achieve any of them.

There is no certain format that the plan has to take, as each plan will be as unique as the skills, interests, and goals of the team member completing it. The plan can be as simple as just a few bullet points to outline their priorities and the follow-up actions they are going to take. Some team members may wish to create a more elaborate plan, which is fine as well. Keep in mind that the ultimate purpose of the written plan is simply for you and your team member to have something to reference to make sure progress is being made on their development priorities.

Coming up with specific career-development ideas can be one of the most difficult aspects of creating a development plan. Many organizations do not define or offer specific developmental opportunities for team members, and many team members have never been asked to identify opportunities that will

> HELP YOUR TEAM MEMBERS FOCUS ON THE IDEAS THAT ARE MOST IMPORTANT TO ACHIEVING THEIR GOALS.

help them achieve their long-term career goals. If you and your team member are struggling to come up with specific ideas to pursue, consider making the following suggestions:

1. **Take part in a company task force or special team assignments—** If your organization has created an internal task force or special team to tackle a specific challenge, have your team members who are interested in the issue volunteer to be part of the project. This not only will give them a developmental opportunity but could also help

them raise their profile in the organization, which will help provide them with more opportunities in the future.

2. **Lead a team initiative**—If your team is facing a specific challenge, don't feel like you always have to create the solution. Instead, assign a team member or a group of team members to explore the issue and create recommendations. Not only does this provide development for them but it also ensures all team challenges do not have to be fixed by you alone.

3. **Mentor new team members**—Even if a team member isn't interested in being a coach someday, they may still enjoy mentoring a new team member on certain skills. This can be a good way for a particularly skilled team member to share their knowledge without being responsible for coaching overall. Plus, this team training approach allows new team members to learn different potential approaches to their work from different peers.

4. **Find a mentor**—If a team member is interested in a particular area of the business or developing a skill set with which another leader excels, help them identify and acquire a mentor in this area. Just because you're their coach doesn't mean you have the best knowledge in all the areas where they want to grow, so asking someone else to step in can help them grow in a different way. This mentor can be internal or external to your organization.

5. **Train with other departments or divisions**—Consider setting up cross-divisional training with a leader in another area of the company. You can have your team members shadow their team members when engaged in tasks that are of interest to your team, and then return the favor by having their team members observe your team members at other times.

6. **Attend external training courses**—There are numerous training courses locally and online that your team members can take

on topics of interest or to develop a specific skill set they need to advance in their career. Quick web searches can reveal a number of opportunities. Also, consider looking at community colleges in your area, as they often offer evening classes on a variety of topics of interest to professionals.

7. **Read books or attend webinars**—At times, taking an entire course isn't necessary, so instead consider having your team member read a book or attend a webinar. Again, online searches can reveal lots of opportunities. Also, if the book or webinar is of interest to you, too, consider reading or watching it with them. Their learning will be enhanced by having someone with which to discuss the material. Also, it will be a way to get to know your team member better beyond your day-to-day coaching of them.

8. **Take part in an industry conference**—Having the opportunity to interact and learn from other professionals in your industry can give your team members exposure to information and ideas they don't hear every day. Companies and departments can tend to become an echo chamber, so this is a good way to ensure they're hearing perspectives they may not have heard before.

9. **Leading team meetings**—Again, many of your team members may never want to have a leadership role in the company, but they still may enjoy the opportunity to lead in smaller ways. Having them lead a team meeting can give them the opportunity to share their knowledge and have influence without a formal leadership role.

10. **Become the team expert on a particular topic**—Have your team members develop an in-depth, expert-level knowledge or skill set that's unique among their team members. The act of developing the skill or knowledge will help them grow, and it will also help the team overall, as team members will have a specific person to go to when they have questions in that area.

After the discussion

At the conclusion of the career discussion, it is important to have clearly defined follow-up steps with your team member. These follow-up steps should include your team member's creation of a written career-development plan and identification of how often the two of you will assess progress against this plan. These post-discussion steps give teeth to the coaching activity, so it's more than just a nice conversation; instead, it's an interaction that leads to the development of your team member's career.

WRITE DOWN THE PLAN

After the career discussion is complete, it is important to put the goals you and your team member identify in writing. You want to have a plan to which you can refer back in your follow-up discussions. Plus, the act of writing down goals makes it more likely that your team member will actually work to achieve them. Remember, your team member is the person ultimately responsible for their own career development, so it's critical that they are the one to create and write down the plan.

FOLLOW UP

Have your team member create a plan and use it as their development plan for the next year. But don't forget about it until next year; follow-up is essential. After your team member has created their career-development plan, use your one-to-one meetings to follow up with their progress at least quarterly. This is simply to touch base and check on progress, so it doesn't have to be overly formal. Just review the plan with them. Ask about the actions they've taken in the last ninety days. Ask if they're running into any challenges or roadblocks. Ask if there is anything more you can be doing to help them reach their goals.

The key reason for doing this follow-up is to help hold your team members accountable for their career development. As we discussed, it's easy for day-to-day work to take precedence over longer-term skill and knowledge development; when your team members are busy, they may forget about the career-development work they have committed to do. Without you as an accountability partner, they're more likely to put it on the back burner.

CHALLENGE YOUR TEAM TO GROW

By definition, your team members' career-development plans should push them outside their comfort zone into Complexity. That is, they should be working on gaining or furthering a skill or knowledge that they don't need for their current daily work but that will help them long term. If your team member comes to you with a career-development plan that simply helps them get better at the responsibilities they already have, they need to go back to the drawing board.

The career-development activity should be challenging them to learn and work outside the areas they already know well. They may feel some trepidation or nervousness about tackling the opportunities on their plan—that's to be expected. Frankly, if they're not at least a little uncertain about how and if they will be able to develop themselves in this area, they're probably not really pursuing a stretch opportunity.

As their coach, you need to be the one to challenge your team into Complexity. You cannot define their career interests, goals, or needs, but you can help motivate them to pursue them. In this process, your role is to be a catalyst for your team members. You do this by asking them interesting questions that stimulate their thinking. You do this by helping them identify growth opportunities they are currently not pursuing. And you do this by holding them accountable to executing the plans they put in place. Under your coaching, career development no longer will feel optional. It will feel like a vital part of their success, both now and into the future.

*A Career Development template can be found at www.ecsellinstitute. com/templates

#WhatTeamMembersSay

"My manager will ask me what areas I am interested in regarding career development and encourages me to seek those out. He meets with us one-on-one to show how our personal goals can be met by meeting our professional goals."

—Through the Eyes of the Team survey respondent

Conclusion:
The Four-Step Coaching Process

#WhatTeamMembersSay

"My manager currently treats members of the team inconsistently. She is close and friendly with two of them and spends most of her time chatting with them during the day. She snaps and issues orders at two others on the team and ignores the remaining team members for the most part. Among ourselves we discuss how we wish she would be more consistent with the way she treats people. Everyone deserves to have a manager who is supportive."

—Through the Eyes of the Team survey respondent

CONSIDER A FUTURE BUSINESS environment in which everyone knows that the most important driver of performance and growth is the effectiveness of their leadership team, and each leader has a clear way to quantify and measure the quality of their own work.

The following chart shows the average scores of two companies for a sample of questions from our Through the Eyes of the Team survey. As we do with all clients, we measured the companies' frontline coaches to quantify their coaching quality. The bottom score, in bold, shows the total average coaching score for the entire management team. While companies ABC and XYZ are in the same industry, XYZ produces greater revenue per salesperson, has greater sales growth over the prior year, has lower turnover, and more managers and salespeople are achieving their goals.

	ABC	XYZ
My manager is effective at motivating to greater performance.	70%	82%
My manager holds one-to-one meetings with me at least twice a month.	71%	91%
My one-to-one meetings with my manager are beneficial.	71%	84%
My manager provides documented feedback at least quarterly.	24%	64%
My manager's feedback helps me perform better.	60%	73%
I find great value in the information provided in team meetings.	68%	85%
My manager understands who I am as a person.	58%	75%
Even if it's uncomfortable, my manager is effective at challenging my skills.	57%	71%
Organizational Coaching Quality Score	62%	75%

Now assume you are a salesperson and have been offered a job with company ABC and with XYZ. Your choice seems obvious, as you'd want to work for the company that has the coaches who will create the most growth in you and for the company where you are more likely to hit your sales targets. If you are in a leadership role and both companies are offering you a position, it would also seem an easy decision, as you'd rather work alongside a high-performing team of coaches and in an environment where more managers achieve sales goals. Simply put, XYZ is the more attractive company.

Here's the twist: ABC and XYZ are the same company, measured less than one year apart. So what does this story tell us? Any organization, regardless of size, can implement a coaching process that leads to greater growth and increased revenue. However, there is a huge challenge to a change like this. All of a sudden, the coaches are the ones on the hook for delivering results. It's no longer just the frontline team members who are supposed to achieve their goals. The coaches have just as much responsibility, if not more, for executing the activities and behaviors that will deliver the numbers.

This concluding chapter will outline exactly how a coaching process should be implemented and executed in an organization to achieve growth above and beyond what is currently being achieved. We will illustrate the results of multiple companies that were committed and realized consistent growth. We'll also share examples of companies that weren't as successful because we all know that is reality too. We will be candid about our experiences and what we have learned about companies that are not afraid of implementing and leading a coaching process that creates Complexity versus those that aren't willing or capable of leading through change and discomfort.

Before we detail the coaching process, we would like to acknowledge that there are other coaching duties we are not covering in this book. Hiring, compensation, planning, and technology implementation are all areas of responsibility for a coach. However, too often these responsibilities are not solely in the hands of the coach, as other departments like human resources, marketing, or finance take on a significant role. Instead, we are focused on the coaching interactions that are clearly within the control of the coach.

Further, our coaching process is solely focused on the coaching interactions that have been shown to lead to better results. While some teams may emphasize activities such as business unit reviews, planning meetings, or pipeline reviews, we've yet to see a measurable performance difference between organizations that conduct these activities regularly and those that do not. Essentially, there's nothing in our data up to this point to indicate that these activities lead to greater discretionary effort. We're not saying they aren't important, but we are focused on the coaching interactions that our research has shown to have a relationship to increased performance.

As we are constantly evaluating which coaching activities and behaviors drive performance, we will continue to look for connections between other coaching interactions and business results.

Finally, you are going to read how we at EcSell Institute implement a coaching process on behalf of our clients. This is not intended to be a self-promotional chapter but rather a way to illustrate how organizations, or departments within any organization, can implement a coaching methodology and the results they can achieve. The four steps we prescribe in this chapter are not so much revolutionary as evolutionary and can be followed by any company willing to execute them.

IMPLEMENTING A COACHING PROCESS

Throughout this book, we have focused on the behaviors and activities that high-growth coaches use to improve team performance. You've learned why both the quantity and quality of coaching matters, and how both affect immediate performance and sustained growth. You've seen disparity in performance between teams, sometimes measured in millions of dollars, who have a high-growth coach versus those whose coach behaves more like a traditional manager. Now it's time to share how a business, division, or team can implement a coaching process that is teachable, measurable, and leads to the creation of more high-growth coaches.

There are four steps our clients have successfully used to implement their coaching processes and create high-growth coaching cultures. These steps are:

1. Measure

2. Educate and train

3. Implement

4. Track and analyze

The steps within the process, though independent, are inextricably linked. You cannot do just one of them and expect growth. As a matter of fact, doing only part of the preceding list could create negative discretionary effort. For example, to begin with *measurement* and not follow with *education and training* is paralyzing. What you've done is shown your coaches their strengths and weaknesses but not offered a way for them to improve. To only educate and train, while attractive and—when done well—exciting, yields minimal long-term impact. Indeed, training research shows that almost everything learned is lost in thirty days without accountability for *implementation* of what was learned. And to do the first three steps without tracking and analyzing results would be analogous to treating a cancer patient without follow-up scans to see if treatments were effective or how to next treat the patient. Simply put, if you want to build a high-growth culture, it takes consistent execution of the entire four-step process.

Step 1: Measure

> *I have been struck again and again*
> *by how important measurement is to improving*
> *the human condition.*
>
> —BILL GATES

Growth in coaching, growth in individuals, growth in outcomes, and growth in sales—these are what our clients are looking for when they embark on a process for improving the execution of coaching within their company. Their growth is of paramount importance to us, too, which is why measurement is the essential first step in our four-step coaching process. Simply put, we begin with measurement to establish a baseline from which to assess progress and improvement over time.

WE BEGIN WITH MEASUREMENT TO ESTABLISH A BASELINE FROM WHICH TO ASSESS PROGRESS AND IMPROVEMENT OVER TIME.

The most important way that we measure our clients' coaching acumen and execution is by administering the Through the Eyes of the Team survey. By asking team members about the consistency and effectiveness of the coaching they receive, we are better able to understand their organization's current coaching environment. This not only helps us establish a baseline of performance but also allows us to tailor our recommendations and coaching process to better meet their needs.

Case Studies: Measurement

The experience of one our clients, a small, specialized pharmaceutical company, is indicative of the benefits that can be achieved through the measurement of coaching. The leadership team had established significant revenue growth goals for the years to come and believed that better mid-level leadership was required to achieve those goals. It decided to partner with us to ensure their coaches had a clearly defined coaching process to employ.

At the outset of our relationship, we surveyed about fifty team members and found that while coaching was happening in the organization, it was not as consistent or high quality as the organization expected. For example, when we asked team members to rate their coach's overall skills as a manager on a scale of one to ten, with ten being high, only 44 percent of them gave their coach a nine or ten, indicating that fewer than half of the team members were highly satisfied with the coaching they were receiving.

Further, coaching was happening too inconsistently. For example, 23 percent of team members said they did one-to-one meetings with their coaches on a weekly basis, 15 percent said every other week, 38 percent said monthly, 16 percent said quarterly, and 8 percent said never. There was no clear standard or expectation, and senior leadership knew they had to be more consistent in their company's execution of this critical coaching practice.

Another information services client had a similar realization when it measured coaching for the first time. For example, when we surveyed more than three hundred team members about how often they received feedback from their manager on their skills, 23 percent said monthly, 17 percent said quarterly, 20 percent said twice a year, 24 percent said annually, and 17 percent said never. Moreover, 60 percent of team members rated the feedback they received as valuable, while the other 40 percent found it to be lacking in quality. It was eye-opening for senior leadership to see that the quantity and quality of the feedback their team members received differed so much depending on who was their coach.

The experience of these two companies is what we see at the measurement stage with many of our clients. Coaching is happening in the organization, but there are many inconsistencies in how often and how effectively it's occurring. Most of the time, our client organizations have never even measured coaching before, so they have no idea of whether it's even occurring or how well it's being received by team members. Finally having this information gives them clarity about their current coaching effectiveness and how they need to improve.

Step 2: Educate and train

*An individual's current skill set is of secondary importance
to their ability to learn new knowledge, skills, and behaviors that
will equip them to respond to future challenges. As a result,
our focus must shift to finding and developing individuals who
are continually able to give up skills, perspectives, and ideas that
are no longer relevant, and learn new ones that are.*

—EXCERPT FROM A CENTER FOR CREATIVE
LEADERSHIP WHITE PAPER

In today's business environment, becoming complacent with your employees' current knowledge, actions, and skill sets is a surefire way to begin the demise of your organization. Continual development—giving up old skills and learning new ones—is absolutely critical to individual and organizational growth. Without moving forward, Stagnation sets in.

Education and training, the second step in the growth coaching process, is a crucial component of a coach's growth journey. But training is not without risk for an organization, with the key danger being starting and stopping with this step. Unfortunately, too many companies view education and training as stand-alone events that will single-handedly provide what is needed to create behavior change and growth outcomes. But as you learned in chapter 1, most people's desire to stay in Order is intense. So despite what is learned at an educational event, that knowledge is often not applied and change is often not implemented. We are certainly not insinuating that organizations shouldn't provide education and training for their people. They just need to follow up and make sure what's learned in the training is actually implemented.

After we've established an organization's coaching baseline with the Through the Eyes of the Team survey, we begin education on best practices. This part of our four-step process helps build emotional commitment to coaching improvement, so that coaches actually want to implement the new ideas they learn. Like all of us, the coaches with whom we work have preconceived notions and ideas that influence their thinking. Through their experiences with their own teams, learning from other leaders, and sometimes even previous management training, they've developed their own beliefs on how to best coach and lead their teams. While their experience can be valuable, we often find that coaches have been taught ineffective ideas about how to drive their team's performance. Even more often, we find that coaches simply haven't been adequately exposed to good modeling or information on how to coach their teams.

This is why we begin the education process by building the coaches' understanding of the importance of coaching. Using a combination of research and case studies, we are able to lay out the factual case of how good coaching can improve the performance of a team. With example after example, we help our clients see how the consistent, effective execution of coaching best practices improves individual and team performance. But even with all the supporting data in the world, coaches aren't going to change their coaching behavior unless they emotionally buy in to the need to do so. This is why we use videos, stories, and interactive exercises to emotionally connect them with the impact of effective coaching.

Next, we cover what the best coaches do to maximize growth of those on their team by looking at how they spend their time and behave differently than less effective coaches. We also introduce the high-growth coaching activities, how we discovered them, and how they can be executed most effectively. This is the roll-up-your-sleeves piece of the education and training, in which coaches share best practices, take part in role-plays, and participate in group exercises to get a feel for how to best execute the coaching activities.

It's important that training and education is not a PowerPoint-and-quiz type of event, as we are trying to get coaches to give up their preconceived notions and make changes in the way they coach. As we've noted multiple times in this book, it's not that the coaching activities we recommend are in and of themselves revolutionary. Rather, it's knowing how and how often to do these activities, as well as having the motivation to actually do them consistently, that are key to more effective coaching. This is why we are especially proud of comments like the following from our coaching academy participants:

> "Coaching is a learned skill, and the academy provides the context and content to develop these key skills."

> "As managers, it's great to see what my organization is already doing and what we're not doing enough. I leave here with a newly strengthened commitment to thorough coaching and relationship building with our team."

> "I am new to management and coaching. I got many ideas from the academy that I can implement. The activities are not revolutionary, but I got the energy from this event to go make actual change in our team. That is very cool!"

For most organizations with whom we work, these are the kind of responses we receive from our education and training participants. It's not uncommon for coaches to declare our coaching academy the best management training they've ever received because of its practical ideas, interactive way of teaching, and focus on creating emotional buy-in with the work they need to do to improve. Unfortunately, though, we don't always get a warm reception.

Case Study: Educate and Train

At one of the first academies we ever executed, we received significant pushback from the participating coaches. The senior leader at this consumer food company had hired us to give his coaches the leadership skills and knowledge he believed they were lacking. Like most coaches, they had been promoted to their roles because they had performed well in individual functions. No one had ever taught them how to lead others, so they were simply relying on their instincts and what they had learned from some mediocre models.

During the day we spent with this team, we shared our usual coaching academy content. While the team was talkative and interactive, they pushed back against nearly every idea we shared, usually with the concern that they didn't have enough time in their days to do this much coaching. On one hand, their concerns were justified, as they did have very busy schedules full of strategy meetings and follow-up on customer issues. On the other hand, they had no justification for why they should continue to focus their time on these activities.

Like most of us, they naturally assumed that their Order was correct because it was familiar to them. If that's what they had been doing for years, it had to be correct, right? As they were so used to and comfortable with their way of doing things, they were not interested in trying a different approach. At the end of the day, even though they insisted they appreciated the information we shared, we felt disappointed because we knew they weren't going to implement any of the ideas.

A few months later, we reconnected with the senior leader who had hired us for the day. He shared with us that his team was still not performing any differently than they had prior to the training, and he was frustrated they hadn't implemented any of our suggestions. He wanted us to come back again for more training, but when we asked what was going to be different this time to ensure execution, he didn't have a response. Ultimately, we told him we didn't want to waste his money if he didn't see his team doing anything different.

We'll be blunt: change is hard. If you are a senior leader who wants your coaches to improve, or if you are a frontline coach who is interested in leading your team more effectively, it's not enough to get excited about the coaching ideas shared in this book. You have to commit to real change, and that takes real work. To us, reading this book is a first step in the process, not dissimilar to attending one of our coaching academies. You may feel as excited about improving your coaching after you finish this book as the participants are at the end of our coaching academies. But the real change happens in the next step. We're glad you're interested in coaching improvement and that you've stayed with us this long. But if you want to really improve or help your team grow, then stick around to learn about step 3.

Step 3: Implement

*Behavior precedes belief—that is, most people must engage in
a behavior before they accept that it is beneficial; then they see the
results, and then they believe that it is the right thing to do. . . .
implementation precedes buy-in; it does not follow it.*

—DOUGLAS B. REEVES

It is easy to say, "Go forth and execute," but if it were that easy, we wouldn't be writing about this step in the process. Unfortunately, a desire for Order reigns supreme. Even after education and training on how to coach better, venturing into Complexity is too uncomfortable. By default, most coaches return to old habits and behaviors.

We've found that the best way to combat this tendency is to create a collaborative implementation environment that is driven by bringing together people who are trying to improve their coaching behavior. We refer to these conference-call gatherings as *implementation huddles*. The focus of these huddles is on the continued sharing of best coaching practices and open discussion of the challenges to overcome in improving coaching. The huddles are jointly led by experts on our client-service team and leaders within our client organizations.

We have also learned the hard way that not all high-growth coaching activities can be implemented at once. Through trial and error, we discovered that implementing one new coaching activity every two months allows coaches to fully integrate each activity before adding another one. We take the time in our implementation huddles to introduce each activity individually, discuss how this activity should be customized to the client organization, and share our tips on how to execute this coaching activity most effectively. Then, the following month, we hold a roundtable discussion with the coaches to gather their feedback on how well the activity is working so far. We have them share stories with one another about what's going well and what can be improved, and we partner with them on further changes needed.

We've found implementation huddles to be helpful for the following reasons:

- They provide coaches the ability to collaborate with one another about what is working and not working.

- They create accountability for implementing the coaching activities, as it's hard for coaches to participate if they have not done the work.

- They reinforce the importance of the coaching process. Unfortunately, too many companies have a reputation of starting something and not following through. Without continual focus, coaches may adopt an attitude of "Just wait; this too shall pass."

- They allow different coaches with different skill levels to collaborate. For example, new coaches typically have different needs than those who have been in the role for years. Top-performing coaches may want to hear more ideas from other top performers. And senior-level coaches may want content geared toward how they coach other coaches.

Implementation huddles did not start out as a key activity in our client work; they were an evolutionary development. For years we couldn't understand why, despite the research and case studies showing that improved coaching led to better results, more coaches weren't adopting the activities with the right frequency and quality. Eventually, the Growth Rings helped us understand the lack of behavior change—most people naturally gravitate to Order. So we decided to introduce the huddles as a way to keep coaches in the Complexity environment.

The huddles had the effect we were hoping they'd have. As we've implemented them with client organizations, we've seen the coaches' quality of coaching interactions improve. Not surprisingly, the coaches who most regularly attend their implementation huddles typically see the biggest increase in their coaching quality scores, as measured by the Through the Eyes of the Team survey.

Case Study: Implementation

A large, publicly traded professional services organization saw a relationship between improved coaching quality and huddle attendance. Its coaches who improved their Coaching Quality Score during the first two years of our partnership were more consistently engaged in monthly huddles. In fact, the coaches who improved were 64 percent more likely to attend huddles than coaches who did not improve.

Another client, a pharmaceutical company, found that coaches who attended at least 89 percent of their monthly huddles had 13 percent higher Coaching Quality Scores than the coaches who attended huddles less consistently. Seeing the impact of huddles on coaching quality, senior leadership made attendance mandatory for their team members. We provided them regular reports with attendance numbers, and the senior leaders used this information to ensure their coaches were participating. As senior leadership got more involved and drove accountability, huddle attendance continued to rise.

We've seen time and time again that providing senior leaders with information about their coaches' engagement with the coaching process helps drive implementation. We build the coaches' buy-in of the importance of coaching with our coaching academy, and then the coaches' implementation huddles help maintain and further their engagement. But there is no substitute for a consistent message coming from the top of the organization on the importance of coaching. As outside experts, we can talk until we are blue in the face about the impact of coaching, but most coaches take their cues from their own leaders. So if senior leadership publicly supports the coaching process and holds their coaches accountable for execution of it, the process is more likely to be successful, plain and simple. This is why step 4 in the process is so essential.

Step 4: Track and analyze

Most decisions are not binary, and there are
usually better answers waiting to be found
if you do the analysis and involve the right people.

—JAMIE DIMON

What would happen if doctors followed evidenced-based medicine best practices only 54 percent of the time? What if engineers provided bridge designs that met only 54 percent of the safety standards they were supposed to meet? In both of these examples, how would their respective

> BECAUSE THE VAST MAJORITY OF COACHES IN
> THE BUSINESS WORLD DON'T HAVE THE DATA
> AND INFORMATION THEY NEED, THEY HAVE BEEN
> UNDERPERFORMING FOR DECADES.

industries and the general public respond to such numbers? It's easy; they'd find the lack of adherence to standards to be completely unacceptable. And because these industries measure quality outcomes and hold people accountable when they are not achieved, this kind of underperformance does not occur.

In most companies we study, coaches are doing only 54 percent of the necessary coaching activities. Further, when they are coaching their team members, 45 percent of coaches are falling short of the coaching quality standards they need to achieve in order to hit their performance goals. And remember, these are the percentages for coaches who work for companies that have committed to a measurable coaching process. Imagine what coaches are doing in companies that have no coaching process, no measurement, and no accountability for coaching.

By measuring coaching quantity and coaching quality, we have become acutely aware that most coaches don't know how their actions and behaviors affect the growth of their teams. They don't know what to do, how often to do it, or how to do it well. Evidence of this can be seen in the numbers listed previously. Because the vast majority of coaches in the business world don't have the data and information they need, they have been underperforming for decades.

Analysis of this kind of coaching information not only allows a story to emerge but also solves a long-standing performance improvement mystery that, up to this point, has never been understood. That is, organizations would see different performance levels from teams, but the only data they could examine to explain this difference was on frontline performers. This information may answer the question in some cases, but without measurement of coach performance, there was a huge unknown variable.

We saw the impact of the coach when we analyzed data across sales departments of our client organizations. Forty-five percent of managers fell below necessary coaching quality standards to hit their sales number. When we considered the average sales goals of these coaches, this translated to $4.1 million left on the table due to inadequate coaching. If you were the CEO at one of these organizations, how would you feel about this? What would your business stakeholders think if you shared this data with them? Unfortunately, the challenge with tracking and analyzing data is that it sometimes yields a story that nobody wants to hear.

While some data and analysis paint a scary picture, many of our client organizations have used this type of analysis to make targeted improvements to their coaching efforts. They've used data to see which coaches are falling behind so they can help them define specific improvement strategies. They've used data to create more accountability for coaching across the entire company. They've used data to gain insights into how coaches are spending their time. They've used data to better understand the impact of good coaching.

Case Study: Track and Analyze

An insurance company that has employed our coaching process across their organization for a number of years saw significant improvement from the use of coaching data. When its leaders began their partnership with us, their goal was simple—they wanted to create better coaches so they could grow their sales. Using our four-step coaching process, they took the necessary steps to measure, educate, implement, and analyze coaching activity and

continued

behavior throughout their sales leadership ranks. They began with strong support and accountability from the senior leader who hired us to help create their coaching process. This leader was passionate about helping her frontline coaches improve, and she was willing to create a culture of Complexity and accountability.

There was significant excitement and engagement at the end of our first coaching academy with this company, but everyone knew the hard work was yet to come. In the first few months of coaching best practice implementation, the frontline coaches struggled to execute coaching at the desired level. After the first year of our partnership, the coaches were averaging only 35 percent completion rates on all the coaching activities across the organization. And while they had improved their Coaching Quality Score from when the Through the Eyes of the Team survey was conducted prior to the coaching process launch, they were still below our client average.

Their senior sales leader knew she had to create more accountability for coaching if she was really going to build a high-growth organization. She took the aggressive step of making coaching part of her coaches' compensation plan. If the coaches executed their coaching at the expected frequency, they were eligible to achieve their full performance bonus. If they did not, they lost a significant percent of their bonus. This was a wake-up call for all the coaches that their boss was serious about making coaching a priority.

Two years later, the company's results had changed drastically. The coaches had more than doubled their completion rate of coaching activities. Their average Coaching Quality Score was 19 percent higher. Most importantly, the company had just achieved its most successful two-year sales results in its history. The senior leader showed how smart she was in doubling down on improved coaching as the way to grow the business.

OBSTACLES TO BECOMING A TOP-PERFORMING, HIGH-GROWTH COACHING ORGANIZATION

If you think most businesses wish to become high-growth coaching organizations, you are correct. But that is like saying most people wish to eat healthier or get fitter. Just like many individuals aren't willing to commit to a diet and workout regimen to be in great physical shape, many companies aren't willing to charge into Complexity and experience the discomfort necessary to build great coaching environments. While perhaps masked in excuses such as "too little budget" or "too many things on our plates right now," what follows are what we have observed as the true obstacles to sustained growth through better coaching.

The executive leader as an obstacle

The most significant performance growth barrier occurs prior to any implementation of a coaching process. It happens when an executive leader hears this coaching growth message, understands the method for implementing a coaching process, and then has the epiphany of how much disruption this will cause. Disruption comes from learning that somewhere between 20 and 40 percent of their managers are inhibiting performance. Disruption comes from realizing that 30 to 45 percent of their existing managers will have to be replaced or redeployed within the next twelve to eighteen months because they will be unwilling to do the activities or behave like a high-growth coach.

Not long ago, we visited with a vice president who, after learning how a coaching methodology can drive growth, said, "Please allow me to paraphrase. What I hear you saying is that I'll now have data that tells me which of my managers is blocking performance versus those that perpetuate it. I'll know who is doing and not doing these high-growth coaching activities and behaviors that lead to growth. But, what I'm also hearing is that I'll likely learn that three to four of my managers aren't cutting the mustard and won't adapt. That means I'll either need to fire or redeploy them." This person then said in all seriousness, "Do you have any idea how much work that will create for me? No, thank you." While this response may shock some, this person at least had the courage to be candid. Many can't admit that they are afraid of the Complexity-caused disruption that will result from trying to create a high-growth coaching culture. Growth is never easy and is often painful because it only occurs in a state of discomfort. Therefore, it takes a strong executive leader who can coach through change.

The frontline coach as an obstacle

While there are plenty of coaches who thrive in an environment of visibility, accountability, and development, there are just as many, if not more, for whom this creates too much discomfort. For too long, organizations have enabled coaches to fly under the radar with poor skills because there was no way to objectively quantify their effectiveness. The discomfort that visibility creates is manifested by coaches in diverse ways, including objections to the survey measurements, objections to the supporting research, or objections to the coaching activities themselves.

> WHEN COACHES EMBRACE DISCOMFORT AND MAKE CHANGES, GROWTH IS THE OUTCOME.

While the high-growth coaching activities are clearly logical for someone in a frontline coaching position, the consistency and frequency of doing them creates anxiety for many. Our data shows that more than half of coaches struggle to hit the expected frequency for their coaching activities. Because we ask organizations to change their coaching routines, Complexity is created, which causes discomfort. When coaches embrace discomfort and make changes, growth is the outcome. For many, however, discomfort leads to avoidance.

LEADERS AT EVERY LEVEL NEED TO LOOK IN THE MIRROR AND ASK THEMSELVES WHETHER THEY ARE AN OBSTACLE TO GROWTH OR A CATALYST FOR IT.

Time as the obstacle

Subjectively, the most frequent excuse we hear should be quickly dismissed. While agreeing that the role of frontline coaches is hugely time-demanding, the top 20 percent don't use time as an excuse. They all have the same twenty-four hours in a day, but the top 20 percent of coaches use those hours differently than the bottom 80 percent, which this book has described in detail. And electing to spend their time differently means their teams account for millions of dollars in greater performance and productivity.

When all the objections and excuses are set aside, the inability of organizations to sustain growth and maximize performance still boils down to a lack of resources, specifically one resource—the human resource. We are not referring to employing more bodies to get more done. We are talking about how organizations employ too many leaders who are unwilling to give up or unlearn what they know. They'd rather keep doing what they've always done than learn something new and enter a state of Complexity to achieve different results. Leaders at every level need to look in the mirror and ask themselves whether they are an obstacle to growth or a catalyst for it. Our data shows us that every coach can improve. This improvement affects not just your own performance but the growth of your entire team.

Simply stated, maximizing growth by creating a high-growth team of coaches is hard. It's not for leadership teams who are unwilling to dive into the challenges that Complexity presents. But as you've learned, growth does not occur unless you are in a state of discomfort. And the good news is the answer to sustained growth is in your control. Whether you are the executive leader within a large organization or the coach of a small cli-ent-service team, the decision to create and sustain growth is now a con-scious decision.

HOW *SHOULD* IT FEEL TO BE COACHED BY YOU?

In the introduction, we asked you to answer a very poignant question: *What does it feel like to be coached by you?* As we close this book, we will now ask a different, yet similar, question: *What* should *it feel like to be coached by you?* Take a moment to write down your response.

_____

_____

_____

Now look back at what you wrote in response to the chapter 1 question. Where is the gap between *how does it feel* and *how should it feel*? Where do you need to improve? What steps can you take to make that improvement? Most important, what changes are you willing to commit to making?

Becoming a great coach is a journey, and the best coaches we study never stop learning or growing. We applaud you for taking an important step in your journey by making the time to read this book and learn more about how you can become a better coach. We hope you implement some of the coaching best practices we shared. Let us know if you do—we are constantly on the lookout for more great coaches to study, and we'd love for you to be one of them.

#WhatTeamMembersSay

"My leader empowers us to try new things, take risks, and pushes us to share our success and failures. He has created a culture that is very collaborative, team-focused and aggressive in our pursuit to win."

—Through the Eyes of the Team survey respondent

About the Authors

BILL ECKSTROM is an executive, entrepreneur, mentor, student, husband, and father. His primary passion is **growth**—especially how coaches and leaders influence the growth and performance of individuals and teams.

This passion inspired Bill to launch EcSell Institute, a research-based organization that works with leaders internationally to help them better understand, measure, and elevate coaching's impact on performance. EcSell's science and programming on the role of the coach has changed behaviors, activities, and performance in diverse industries, from athletic teams to businesses around the world.

Bill began his management career in 2000 at a medical equipment company and climbed the ranks to become US director of sales in just three years. In 2004, Bill accepted a job as senior vice president of business development for a publicly traded health-care organization. By 2008, the organization's stock price had doubled and new sales revenue had grown more than 100 percent. Later that same year, he founded EcSell Institute.

As a result of his experiences, his company's findings, and his public speaking skills, Bill's work as a keynote speaker is internationally renowned. Audiences have called him "profoundly authentic," "highly entertaining," and more. Bill is proudest of the fact that the material he presents is rooted in EcSell's research and hard data—no motivational fluff. He has presented to hundreds of groups and is a popular guest on podcasts and shows around the world. Bill was invited to the TEDx stage in 2017, and his talk entitled "Why Comfort Will Ruin Your Life" was the fastest-growing TEDx Talk in the history of the event when it was released.

Growth is also what inspires Bill's philanthropic life, especially his involvement in therapy-dog work. He and his Labrador, Aspen, work together at senior living homes, children's hospitals, and anywhere the presence of Aspen's wagging tail and soft soul can bring a smile.

Bill's home is in Nebraska, where he lives with his wife, Kerstin. Together they have three children—Will Jr., Claire, and Maddie.

SARAH WIRTH has twenty years of experience in employee assessment, leadership development, sales executive coaching, and customer service.

She began her career as a talent analyst for an international human resources firm, where she coached leaders in organizations ranging from small not-for-profits to Fortune 500 companies. When named chair of leadership consulting and a member of the senior operations team, she helped lead the organization to a 65 percent increase in revenue. In 2009, she joined a publicly traded organization as the vice president of client service, increasing client contract retention by 36 percent.

In 2011, Sarah came on board with EcSell Institute as vice president of client services, where she oversees client retention and all aspects of sales coaching, leadership, and management research. Under Sarah's leadership, EcSell Institute's client retention rate has grown to over 94 percent.

Sarah has a passion for leadership and its impact on the performance of teams. She takes an analytical approach to understanding the skills and talents of high-performing sales leaders and is constantly providing EcSell Institute clients with new methods for leading and coaching.

Sarah has presented to executives from across the globe with organizations such as Mercedes-Benz, Estée Lauder, Ritz-Carlton, The Cheesecake Factory, and many more. Her expertise in coaching and leadership, combined with her fact-based and commonsense approach to their application, makes her a sought-after presenter at any event.

Sarah has a BA from the University of Nebraska, holds a JD from the University of Michigan Law School, and is a member of the Nebraska Bar Association. She has served as a legal advisor for many organizations, specifically in the areas of contract, employment, and intellectual property law. She lives in Kansas City with her husband, Mike, and two sons, Miles and Emmett.